force 11 on the Beaufort scale, i.e. up to 75 miles per hour. Many ships lost their places in the convoy, lost touch with the convoy commodore, and suffered heavy weather damage which caused long delays in port while they were repaired. The one redeeming feature was that the U-boats' activities were also severely restricted by the weather, and few merchant ships were lost in November and December of that year.

For people who spend their lives close to a coastline, the sound of the sea can be serene and soothing, even soporific, as it gently stirs the pebbles on the foreshore and slaps against

below: HMCS *Swansea*, a Canadian River Class Frigate active in the Battle of the Atlantic from 1943 to 1945. *Swansea* was involved in the hunting and destruction of four German U-boats.

Of the enemies of the merchant sailors, the sea itself was often the most frightening, threatening, unpredictable and unforgiving; below: Some 267 Flower-class corvettes served with the British Royal Navy, the Royal Canadian Navy, and the United States Navy (through the Lend-Lease agreement) in the Second World War. Other Flower-class corvettes saw action with the Free French Naval Forces, the Royal New Zealand Navy, the South African Navy, the Royal Norwegian Navy, the Royal Indian Navy and the Royal Hellenic Navy. HMCS *Sackville*, berthed in Halifax, Nova Scotia, is the only example of the class preserved as a museum ship.

the rocks; at other times, when an incoming tide is allied with high winds, the sea can show a more ferocious aspect of its nature. Then, it can rear, pour over the promenades, and lash against the piers. But it is not until a man goes aboard a ship and ventures far from land, that he begins to realise what a raging monster the sea can sometimes be, towering and cascading, with a noise like nothing else on earth.

Some will thrill to the experience, to the sound, sight and feel of it; some will be awestruck, even terrified; others will simply suffer *mal de mer*, and devoutly wish they were not there. The ordinary merchant sailor, and his comrade in the Navy, will just accept it as a normal part of life.

In July 1941, a group of survivors had been adrift for eighteen days, and their small supply of water had run out. A Lascar deckhand lay in the bottom of the lifeboat, clearly dying of thirst. Seated beside him, an engineer decided that nothing could be lost by attempting an experiment. He stirred a little of his precious toothpaste into a mug half-full of sea-water, raised the Lascar's head and persuaded him to drink. After an hour, the Lascar opened his eyes, sat up, and in due course recovered sufficiently to take his turn at paddling the boat. Later, the toothpaste manufacturers were asked if their product contained an ingredient which might make sea-water potable. The reply was: "Not so far as our chemists are aware."

The way to be popular on board a lifeboat, if and when the emergency arose, was to try to remember, before you left the ship, to snatch up something that might stand you and your shipmates in good stead: a packet of biscuits, a tin of sardines, first aid dressings, and as many bottles of beer as you could find. Any man with a mouth-organ could be sure of being *persona grata* on the boat. That was in the early days and by the autumn of 1942, it had become clear that the equipment in many merchantmen's lifeboats was inadequate to meet the demands of an escalating war. Men had survived the sinking of their ships only to die slowly of cold, thirst, starvation or exposure in a hopelessly ill-equipped craft. Investigations showed that certain ship owners had not even seen fit to meet the most basic of requirements for the safety of their crews. The rules were then officially examined and enforced, and they included the replacement of the bulky, standard life-jackets by buoyant, yellow waistcoats with battery-operated red lights (an idea inspired by the equipment used by London bus conductors for inspecting tickets in the blackout), and the provision of brightly-coloured, weatherproof suits.

Other equipment to be carried in lifeboats included water-pumps (to obviate baling), apparatus for distilling sea-water, fishing lines, concentrated food in tablet form, lamps which lit automatically on contact with the water, smoke signals and rockets, folding ladders, sidescreens and canopies, rain-catchers, needles and twine, whistles, signalling mirrors, oil for massaging, compasses and charts. Rations were increased and water stocks trebled. "They're putting so much stuff in now" was the laconic reaction of the hardened seaman, "that there's no room for us." Lifeboats had skates fitted to their bottoms, so they would slide down the side of a listing ship, and rafts were made reversible, in case (as often happened) they went into the water upside down. Further regulations required that every ocean-going ship's crew should include three radio officers, and that at least one of her lifeboats should be powered by a motor, with sufficient fuel for 160 miles. Tanker crews were issued with flame-resistant overalls and hoods.

Seventeen hands from a ship that was torpedoed a few degrees north of the Equator in the South Atlantic survived in some style for twelve days on a raft. Their provisions included bis- cuits, corned beef and condensed milk, and to these the young commander of the U-boat which had sunk them added cigarettes, chocolate and a bottle of cognac, before bidding them farewell. In the course of their voyage, two men contrived to seize a turtle by its fins and to hoist it aboard. After due consideration, however, they decided to return the startled creature to the deeps. Later, having fashioned hook and line, and with flying fish for bait, they caught themselves a shark, which they boiled with salt water in a chocolate tin. The meat, so cooked, was white and firm, and pronounced entirely edible. When picked up by a Spanish freighter, all the survivors were in fair condition, apart from sunburn and salt water blisters.

The weather took no sides in the Atlantic battle, it was fair or foul to all according to its mood. The U-boat crews could escape the worst of it while they stayed at depth, but once they surfaced, they were liable to suffer more than most. Herbert Werner described how it was in January 1943, when *U-230* joined a wolfpack in the North Atlantic. "Water that poured in through the open hatch and sloshed around our feet, and the high humidity within the hull caused food to rot, the skin to turn flabby, and our charts to dissolve. The smell was brutal. The extra fuel we carried in our bilges sent out a penetrating stench; our clothes reeked of it and our food took on the taste of oil and grease . . . the sea boiled and foamed and leaped continually under the lash of gales that chased one another across the Atlantic from west to east. *U-230* struggled through gurgling whirlpools, up and down mountainous seas; she was pitched into the air by one towering wave, caught by another and buried under tons of water by yet another. The cruel winds whipped across the wild surface at speeds of up to 150 miles per hour, whistling in highest treble and snarling in the lowest bass."

The years of World War Two produced unique spectacles which anyone who saw them will always remember. No-one can forget the sight of the night sky above a city under air attack, lit by searchlights and twinkling bursts of flak, of a battleship, heavy with armament, setting out from port, of a division of USAAF heavy bombers heading east in combat formation from an assembly point in East Anglia. Another unforgettable sight, was of a major convoy, steadily advancing with ensigns fluttering, creamy bow waves, spreading washes, the long, low tankers in the centre columns, fast-moving destroyers and sloops patrolling the flanks, and a great, grey cruiser or a carrier in their midst—all set against an awesome, ever-changing seascape.

There is nothing more enticing, disenchanting and enslaving, than the life of the sea.
—from *Lord Jim* by Joseph Conrad

The sea hates a coward.
—from *Mourning Becomes Electra* by Eugene O'Neill

It is difficult to row in a heavy sea. The men can last at it about fifteen minutes, and by making every stroke count, can perhaps get a half mile from the ship. Be sure you do not start pulling on the oar before it is in the water. Keep your eye on the stroke oar on each side of the boat. Put the weight of your body on the oar. In a boat properly rowed a thrumming noise issues from the oars and gives a sense of timing.
—from *HOW TO ABANDON SHIP* by Phil Richards and John J. Banigan

Ports are necessities, like postage stamps or soap, but they seldom seem to care what impressions

they make.
—from *Arrival At Santos* by Elizabeth Bishop

How holy people look when they are sea-sick!
—from *Notebooks* by Samuel Butler

The dragon-green, the luminous, the dark, the serpent-haunted sea.
—from *The Gates of Damascus, West Gate*, by James Elroy Flecker

We went southwards through the minefields and then into the English Channel where we saw overhead great flights of cargo gliders being towed over to the continent by planes for what we found out later was the start of the Normandy Invasion. Our first call back in Canada was at Halifax where we anchored in the very deep water of Bedford Basin to discharge our ballast. I found this operation very interesting as they dropped a little bulldozer into each hold and it pushed our pit shale ballast into piles that a crane grab could bite into.

The grab rushed up out of the hold and just flung its load into the harbour which was amply deep enough to swallow all that we had carried over the ocean.
—Robert Atkinson

Roll on, thou deep and dark blue Ocean—roll! / Ten thousand fleets sweep over thee in vain;
Man marks the earth with ruin—his control / Stops with the shore.
—from *Childe Harold's Pilgrimage* by Lord Byron

The Canadian corvette HMCS *Barrie* operating in the heavy seas of the North Atlantic in 1941.

IMAGES OF WAR

MERCHANT SAILORS AT WAR 1943-1945 BEATING THE U-BOAT

RARE PHOTOGRAPHS FROM WARTIME ARCHIVES

PHILIP KAPLAN

WITH JACK CURRIE

Pen & Sword
MARITIME

First printed in Great Britain in 2015 by
Pen & Sword Maritime
an imprint of
Pen & Sword Books Ltd.
47 Church Street
Barnsley,
South Yorkshire
S70 2AS

A CIP record for this book is available from the British Library.

ISBN 978 1 78 346 3053

Printed and bound in Malta
By Gutenberg Press Ltd

Pen & Sword Books Ltd incorporates the Imprints of Pen & Sword Aviation, Pen & Sword Family History, Pen & Sword Maritime, Pen & Sword Military, Pen & Sword Discovery, Wharncliffe Local History, Wharncliffe True Crime, Wharncliffe Transport, Pen & Sword Select, Pen & Sword Military Classics, Leo Cooper, The Praetorian Press, Remember When, Seaforth Publishing and Frontline Publishing.

For a complete list of Pen & Sword titles please contact Pen & Sword Books Limited
47 Church Street, Barnsley, South Yorkshire, S70 2AS, England

E-mail: enquiries@pen-and-sword.co.uk
Website: www.pen-and-sword.co.uk

Contents

All reasonable efforts have been made to trace the copyright holders of all material used in this book. The author apologizes for any omissioins. Reasonable efforts will be made in future editions to correct any such omissions. The author is grateful to the following people for the use of their published and/or unpublished material, or for their kind assistance in the preparation of this book: Christine Ammer, Jack Armstrong, Brooks Atkinson, Robert Atkinson, Francis Bacon, G.S. Bagley, Malcolm Bates, Charles Bishop, William Bourner, Samuel Butler, George Gordon Lord Byron, Winston S. Churchill, Samuel T. Coleridge, Joseph Conrad, Jack Currie (for his text), Peter Donnelly, Dwight D, Eisenhower, Joseph Fabry, The Falkirk Herald, James E. Flecker, Sir Humphrey Gilbert, Kenneth Grahame, Charles Graves, Peter Guy, H.G. Hall, Cyril Hatton, Thom Hendrickson, Charles Hill, Samuel Johnson, Joseph J. Kaplan, Neal B. Kaplan, Ernest J. King, Rudyard Kipling, Collie Knox, Frank Knox, John Lester, Steven Levingston, Peter Lewis, Grant MacDonald, Peter MacDonald, Otto Marchica, Edwin Markham, John Masefield, Wilson McArthur, Nicolas Monsarrat, Eugene O'Niell, John Palmer, A.H. Pierce, C.H. Rayner, Phil Richards, Francis Rockwell, S. Roskill, Thomas Rowe, Owen Rutter, Carl Sandburg, Leonard Sawyer, Frank Shaw, Neil Thompson, Harry S. Truman, Nancy Byrd Turner, Jack Thompson, Peter Wakker, Herbert Werner, Robert Westall, W. Whiting, J.W.S. Wilson, Woodrow Wilson, Roger P. Wise, E. Withers.

According to the myths of ancient Rome, Jupiter, as ruler of the universe, decided to allot certain parts pf planet Earth to his brothers, and he assigned the sea to Neptune (or Poseidon, as the Greeks would have it.) From that time on, Neptune tended to eschew Olympus in favour of his new domain, and to make his home within its depths. It was believed that he could call up the wildest storms, or quell them, according to his whim—a facility of which the poet Homer was to write. "He spake, and round about him called the clouds / And roused the ocean—wielding in his hand The trident—summoned all the hurricanes / Of all the winds, and covered the earth and sky / At once with mists, while from above the night / Fell suddenly."

One Merchant Navy skipper put it less poetically: "You can't beat the sea, it's stronger than you are." The proof was always there. Without any form of assistance from the enemy's mines or bombs, guns or torpedoes, King Neptune contrived that approximately 1,000 Allied ships, should be lost in the course of World War Two.

There were sometimes twelve convoys at a time crossing the Atlantic, with over 20,000 men engaged. They might be under escort by warships or, when they were in what was known as "the Atlantic gap" or "the graveyard", they might not. Always, they were restricted to moving at the speed of the slowest ship among them. For Able Seaman Thomas Rowe, who served on merchant ships throughout the war, "the North Atlantic was the worst ocean I ever travelled, with ferocious storms and mountainous waves, the power and weight of which was really terrifying, especially at night when you could only see the flourescence on the crests as they reared up alongside the ship. Nearing the coast of America or Canada you usually ran into fog, which added to the hazards of sailing in convoy. It was not uncommon to be fogbound for two or three days in that area."

There were fifty-three days in the last three months of 1941 when the winds measured

The oceans and their perils played no favourites in the war years. Riding out the rollers on the surface was as uncomfort-able, if not more so, for the crews of submarines as it was for those of any other warship type. The saving grace was the ability of the submarine captain to submerge and avoid the worst of the sea conditions.

Tramp

The tramp steamer of the 1930s, now almost extinct, was basically a vessel with a box-shaped hull and a sparse superstructure, always built for maximum capacity, and low-powered for economic operation. Normally a tramp displaced less than ten thousand tons and steamed at about ten knots. Many were launched at shipyards in the northeast of Britain, where there was a long tradition of shipbuilding. A tramp could be away from home for perhaps two years, sailing no fixed routes, and always available to the highest bidder for carrying cheap and easily-handled bulk commodities from and to any port at any time. Crew accommodation in a tramp was of a basic sort. Typical were those which plied from Wales, carrying coal and returning with timber, ore and grain. A liner, on the other hand, was a cargo ship, with a normal displacement of between ten and fifteen thousand tons, and two or three decks to facilitate loading and stowage. She could also carry passengers, and would run to a schedule on an advertised route between fixed places, at a speed some five knots faster than a tramp.

The crew of a liner normally wore uniform, the crew of a tramp did not. If such a thing would be suggested, a tramp sailor's reaction would probably have been: "What, wear fancy dress for going to sea? Not likely, mate."

Big items of cargo, such as locomotives, Sherman tanks and two-engined bombers, often had to be carried on the decks, because the hatches were not big enough to lower them into holds.

In 1940, and for some years after, the armament on most merchant ships consisted of four-inch and twelve-pounder guns that dated from World War One, and there were certain difficulties in mounting them on board. The merchantmen were not designed to carry weaponry, and sight-lines were obstructed by rigging, derricks, and other fixtures. There was also the problem, when guns were being mounted, of allowing for the top weight and balance of the ship. The armament was originally manned by the Merchant Navy men themselves, after a three-day course in gunnery with the Royal Navy; later, trained gunners of the DEMS (Defensive Equipment Merchant Ships) took over, and by 1944 they numbered 35,000, including 13,000 soldiers of the Marine Regiment of Artillery. They were serving on 7,000 ships, from the biggest liners to the smallest tugs. Commanded by a Petty Officer or senior NCO, the DEMS then formed the nucleus of a ship's gun crew and trained other seamen to support them. Their counterparts in the American Merchant Marine were the Naval Guard, led by an Ensign (the equivalent of a Royal Navy Midshipman) who, because of his short, intensive training, was sometimes referred to as a "ninety-day wonder."

To keep a tramp on station in a convoy was a formidable task. If she fell astern, or wandered off her course, she could seldom make the speed to regain her place. That might put the Commodore in something of a quandary: should he slow the convoy down, order a dog-leg, or leave her to her fate? The chances were that he had told the masters at his conference before the convoy sailed "I will not leave you alone," and he would stay true to that.

Tramp steamers formed the bulk of the vessels on the Russian convoys, and in the Arctic winter, from mid-December until late in May, they needed ice-breakers to make a way for them. Furthermore, they had to maintain a position close astern of the breaker, or the ice would have reformed.

The tramp seamen bore almost half the casualties sustained by the Merchant Navy during World War Two—most of them in the Atlantic battle.

On 11 January 1940, Jack Armstrong from Hull nervously climbed a rope ladder from a lighter to the deck of the SS *Dalesmoor*, a Walter Runciman Line tramp which was lying at anchor in Liverpool Bay. His fibre suitcase, containing two white jackets and a suit of dungarees, all provided by the owners, plus his worldly possessions, was hoisted up after him. He was seventeen years old and small for his age, timid and bespectacled, and he had never been to sea. Nevertheless, the engineer's mess boy had failed to present himself, and Jack was his replacement. He found himself in charge of a tiny pantry and a mess room big enough for three of *Dalesmoor*'s engineers at any one time. His supply of water had to be fetched from below in the engine room, and he soon learned to hurry up a few rungs of the ladders as

below: Taking cargo aboard the *Jussi H* in Halifax; right :A coal-loading facility in wartime Halifax.

below: A British convoy steaming on the North Atlantic; centre: Cyril Hatton who was a Leading Telegraphist in HMS *Snowflake* in the Second World War; right: Peter Wakker who served as an engineer aboard the SS *Triton* in the war years.

the ship's bows fell in the water, and he had to hold on hard as she rose and the force of gravity tried to tear the bucket from his hand.

"The catering staff," said Armstrong, "consisted of the Chief Steward, who also served the Captain, and an assistant who looked after the navigation officers, me, and the cook, who fed the crew of thirty-five. There was no refrigerator, only a cold store, where the food slowly deteriorated as the ice melted. Then we were reduced to salted meat or corned beef. Like most old ships, the *Dalesmoor* was alive with cockroaches, which fell from the steam pipes into the stew-pans on the cooking range, while the weevils and maggots got into the flour from which the cook made bread. You could pick them out, but there were times when you were so hungry that you didn't bother any more. All the food was severely rationed, and the Runciman Line were well-known for 'starvation boats', as were many other tramp lines. The old seamen knew them all.

The Captain and the Chief Steward were responsible for victualling the ship, and everybody knew that they paid the chandlers first-class prices for third-class provisions, and shared the difference between them."

Armstrong's first voyage with the *Dalesmoor*, in May 1940, was west-bound to Canada. "Convoys didn't always have an escort in those days, and we took a zig-zag course, but our main protection from the enemy was the weather, which in winter was severe. It was a fearsome sight to see a huge wave towering over you, then crashing down on the ship and right over the bridge. It was surprising how quickly you learned to walk with your legs apart and

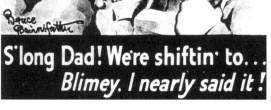

S'long Dad! We're shiftin' to...
Blimey. I nearly said it!

TALK KILLS

DIG FOR VICTORY

"Keep
it
under
your
hat!"

CARELESS TALK COSTS LIVES

YOUR TALK
MAY KILL YOUR COMRADES

Keep mum
she's not so dumb!

CARELESS TALK COSTS LIVES

DON'T WASTE
BREAD!

SAVE TWO SLICES
EVERY DAY and
Defeat the 'U' Boat

Denkt an Eure Kinder!

to roll with the ship, so you could walk the deck without hanging onto the rails—like walking up and down hills and sideways as well. Sometimes, the seas put the galley fires out, and then we had to be down to hardtack—ship's biscuits, that you had to tap on the table to knock the weevils out.

"With the ship in ballast, the screw came out of the water when the bows went down, and the whole ship shuddered. The engineers worked hard, putting on the revs when the screw was in the water, and cutting the power when it was out. There were days when we hardly moved because of that, just bobbing like a cork. It took us a month to do a fortnight's voyage, and we completely lost the convoy. All the engine room activity meant that two engineers had to be there all the time, and they were exhausted. Even the Chief had to turn to, and he was about seventy, with poor eyesight, like me. The voyage took so long that the food ran out and we were back on hardtack.

"Taking early morning tea to the Second Engineer was rather scary. He never woke up to a vocal call, and if I shook him he came out of his bunk fighting. I think it was from dealing with him that I learned to fear the war. We loaded with grain at St John in Newfoundland, where the ladies were very good to the crew, providing us with 'comforts' they had hand-knitted—Balaclavas, scarves, mittens, gloves and sea-boot stockings. We assembled at Halifax with a convoy of twelve ships, again without an escort, and we were soon attacked by a U-boat. There was a tremendous explosion, and I dashed on deck to see the ship next to us in the column, with its stern sticking up. She was loaded with ore and sank quickly, and there

Keep your guns manned and fingers on the trigger.
Do not straggle. We cannot give you any protection if
you drop astern.
—from *Life Line* by Charles Graves

was a second explosion with a great gust of steam and water as the boilers blew up. The order was given to scatter, which was our method of defence then, and as we moved away, increasing speed, there were two more explosions.

"We made our own way after that, eventually joining up with two other ships before we were met by two corvettes two days out from England. There were all kinds of craft in the Thames, and it was only then that we learned about Dunkirk. No radios were allowed on board, and the ship's radio was only switched on at certain times for distress messages, incoming orders and the like, so we had no news of what was going on in the war, either at sea or on the land. We didn't know about the heavy bombing raids, and when I went home to Hull, I was appalled at the damage. The city was virtually dead, and my family had moved to Huddersfield."

Navy Department, Washington / Confidential / 30 March 1942
From: The Secretary of the Navy
To: All Ships:
1. It is the policy of the United States government that no U.S. Flag merchant ship be permitted to fall into the hands of the enemy.
2. The ship shall be defended by her armament, by maneuver, and by every available means as long as possible. When, in the judgement of the Master, capture is inevitable, he shall scuttle the ship. Provision shall be made to open sea valves, and to flood holds and compart-

Oh, where are you going to, all you Big Steamers, With England's own coal, up and down the salt seas? 'We are going to fetch you your bread and your butter, your beef, your pork, and mutton, eggs, apples and cheese.
—from *Big Steamers* by Rudyard Kipling

We are as near to heaven by sea as by land!
—from *Hakluyt's Voyages* by Sir Humphrey Gilbert

There is a tide in the affairs of men, Which, taken at the flood, leads on to fortune; / Omitted, all the voyage of their life / Is bound in shallows and in miseries. / On such a full sea we are now afloat, / And we must take the current when it serves. / Or lose our ventures.
—from *Julius Caesar* by William Shakespeare

ments adjacent to machinery spaces, start numerous fires and employ additional measures available to ensure certain scuttling of the vessel.

3. In case the Master is relieved of command of his ship, he shall transfer this letter to his successor, and obtain a receipt for it.

—Frank Knox

In Liverpool alone, 30,000 dock workers handled more than 75,000,000 tons of cargo during the war. More than 4,500,000 troops moved through the port of Liverpool between 1939-45.

After a short leave, the Merchant Navy Pool instructed me to travel to Scotland where I boarded the *Queen Mary* for passage to New York. There I spent three or four weeks in the St George Hotel in Brooklyn whilst waiting for the *Empire Battleaxe* to be built. We were treated exceptionally well in New York. All the USO clubs, women's voluntary organisations, etc., had something to offer . . . coffee and doughnuts, dancing, and one or two women's organisations gave us a shoe box parcel filled with all manner of useful items . . . hand-knitted pullovers, socks, Balaclavas. We were also given free tickets to cinemas and theatres. I was given a job to relieve the boredom of waiting for the ship to be finished. I worked as a bus-boy at Stouffer's restaurant in Grand Central Station. I was paid thirty dollars a week plus tips.

—Charles Bishop, steward/cook

convoy: a protective escort. The word entered the English language as long ago as the fourteenth century, coming from the Latin *conviare*, to accompany, to travel with, via the Old French *conveier* or *convoier*, to accompany. However, it acquired the specific connotation of protection only during the sixteenth century.

During World War One, beginning with the sinking of the passenger liner Lusitania in 1915, German submarine attacks on Allied shipping became an ever-increasing hazard, so that Allied troop and supply ships were obliged to travel in convoys protected by destroyers. The same practice continued during World War Two. Both as a noun and as a verb, convoy retains the military sense of protection against the enemy, but it also is used in civilian affairs, as, for example, a motorcycle convoying a visiting dignitary.

—from *Fighting Words* by Christine Ammer

Implacable I, the implacable Sea; / Implacable most when most I smile serene—Pleased, not appeased, by myriad wrecks in me.

—from *John Marr and Other Sailors* by Herman Melville

The Sea is Woman, the Sea is Wonder—Her other name is Fate!

—from *Virgilia* by Edwin Markham

The sea speaks a language polite people never repeat. It is a colossal scavenger slang and has no respect.

—from *Complete Poems* by Carl Sandburg

This wartime dance band served as one of many entertainments available to the sailors of the Merchant Navy when they visited Halifax, Nova Scotia, in WW2.

The sea is a great maker of men, men of courage and of grit, men of authority and resource, men of nerve, strength and muscle fitness. For fools she has no use; nor for slackers, nor yet the timid. These she either breaks or casts aside.
—Joseph Conrad

Among the most popular spots with sailors of the Merchant Navy during their brief stays in Halifax was the Green Lantern restaurant and soda fountain, typical of such facilities in the period of the war years.

When any vessel goes down from any cause in wartime, the sea nearby is frequently littered with survivors clinging to life and praying for rescue.

R. M. S "LUSITANIA"   SATURDAY, JUNE 27, 1914

Menu

Hors d'œuvres—Variés
Canapé—Levasseur   Tartelettes—Moscovite

Chicken Okra   Crême Algerienne

Sea Bass—Egyptienne   Fried Filet of Flounder

Grenadins á la Florentine   Biscantins—St. Germain

Sirloin & Ribs of Beef
Haunch of Mutton—Boulangére   Turkey—Mephisto
York Ham & Spinach—Sherry Sauce

Green Peas   Rice   Fried Egg Plant
Boiled, Mashed & Persillées Potatoes

Asperges—Sauce Divine
Salade de Saison

Pouding Normande
Gâteau Vanille   Petits Fours   Rhubarb Tart
Gelée au Madere

Lemon & Coffee Ices

Dessert   Café

TO ORDER FROM THE GRILL (15 Minutes)
Sirloin Steaks   Spring Chicken   Mutton Chops

From the days of the First World War, through present conflicts, graphic art has played a major part. Here are examples.

In August 1935, American President Franklin Roosevelt's Depression-era New Deal Works Progress Administration launched the Federal Art Project. Through 1943, its artists created more than 200,000 posters, murals, and paintings, many of them in aid of the American war effort in WW2.

Posters and other wartime graphics of American origin.

A FEW
CARELESS WORDS
MAY END IN THIS–

Many lives were lost in the last war through careless talk
Be on your guard! Don't discuss movements of ships or troops

U.S. FOOD ADMINISTRATION

EAT MORE
CORN, OATS AND RYE PRODUCTS — FISH AND POULTRY — FRUITS, VEGETABLES AND POTATOES BAKED, BOILED AND BROILED FOODS

EAT LESS
WHEAT, MEAT, SUGAR AND FATS

TO SAVE FOR THE ARMY AND OUR ALLIES

BUNDLES FOR BRITAIN

We Can Do It!

Corvette

The Flower-class corvette, K181, HMCS *Sackville*, is the last of the 123 modern corvette warships built for the Canadian Navy's use in the Second World War. Canada's oldest fighting ship, she has served as that nation's official Naval memorial since 1985 and is appropriately berthed in Halifax, Nova Scotia, the east coast port that was the most important assembly point and destination for the Allied convoys during the Battle of the Atlantic. Moored alongside the Maritime Museum of the Atlantic in Halifax, *Sackville* has been restored to her 1944 condition.

Sackville was laid down at the Saint John Shipbuilding and Drydock Company of Saint John, New Brunswick in 1940, as the second Flower-class corvette ordered by the Royal Canadian Navy. She was launched in May 1941 and was commissioned into the Navy on 30 December 1941. Her first commanding officer was Lieutenant W.R. Kirkland, RCNR, who was appointed on the day of her commissioning. Lieutenant Kirkland was discharged in March 1942 as "unsuitable" following a poor working-up trip to Newfoundland in late February. It was reported that Kirkland had been unable to perform his duties and was abusive to his officers. Assigned to go to the rescue of survivors from the sunken Greek ship *Lily*, *Sackville* was then unable to relocate the convoy, ONS 68, she had been escorting. Her First Lieutenant then relieved Kirkland and assumed command. Her initial crew was posted to other RCN warships and was replaced by the trained crew of HMCS *Baddeck* under Lieutenant-Commander Alan Easton who took command of *Sackville* in April 1942.

In mid-May, *Sackville* and two other Canadian corvettes, *Galt* and *Wetaskiwin*, were assigned to the Mid-Ocean Escort Force, replacing three corvettes going for refit. In August, she fought in several savage actions while escorting convoy ON 115 when the convoy was attacked by two successive U-boat "wolfpacks" near the Newfoundland coast. Heavy fog prevented Allied air cover, but the corvette managed to catch the submarine *U-43* on the surface and, as the *U-43* dived, *Sackville* hit it with a series of depth charges, severely damaging it. The sub limped back to Europe for repairs. The next day *Sackville* did the same to the *U-552*, also catching it on the surface, thus putting two U-boats out of action and helping considerably to enable the forty-one-ship convoy to make the voyage with the loss of only two ships. There followed an extensive refit in Liverpool for the now battle-hardened corvette which then continued her vital escort work through the end of June 1944.

While her boilers were being cleaned, a major leak was discovered which could not be successfully repaired, and *Sackville* was declared unsuitable for further convoy escort work. In late August she was reassigned in a training role. In her wartime service, she had sailed in escort of thirty Trans-Atlantic convoys.

By 1979, HMCS *Sackville* was the only remaining Flower-class corvette and she was transferred to the Canadian Naval Memorial Trust which restored her to basic 1944 appearance making it possible for her to serve in the summer months as a museum ship. She winters in the naval dockyard at CFB Halifax under the care of the Royal Canadian Navy Atlantic Fleet.

The British Flower-class of corvettes numbered 267 warships during the Second World War, operating mainly in the anti-submarine escort role. They were all named after flowers. These corvettes were considered slow for a warship and were lightly armed, intended solely for anti-submarine warfare. Originally planned to be small convoy escort ships, they could be produced quickly and cheaply to be deployed in large numbers. Though intended mainly for coastal convoy work, their long range suited them for mid-ocean escort force work.

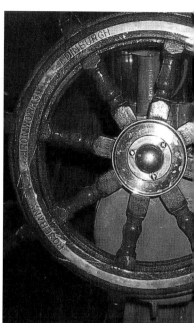

Scenes of HMCS *Sackville*, now a memorial museum ship moored near the Maritime Museum of the Atlantic in Halifax, Nova Scotia, Canada; upper right: Robert Seager who served in the Canadian corvette, K223 in the Second World War.

left: Rear Admiral P.H. Aboyneau aboard a Free French corvette in 1942; below: Free French leader General Charles de Gaulle decorating a French corvette officer; right: Officers in the wardroom of a Free French corvette; other images of the corvette HMCS *Sackville*.

Few warships epitomize the Atlantic war more than the lowly Flower-class corvette. An auxiliary vessel hastily built to mercantile standards and pushed into service by the score, with poor equipment and green crews, the corvette was hardly a match for Germany's U-boat fleet. But the humble corvette made Allied victory in the Atlantic possible: they allowed the convoy system to be extended throughout the North Atlantic and they provided the 'forces of position' which freed better-equipped anti-submarine vessels to do their job. Perhaps most important of all, the unpretentious corvette—especially the first 54 of the 1939-40 building program that carried Canada's war at sea until 1943—defined the formative experience of the Canadian navy and shaped its role for the next 50 years. The ship that launched the Royal Canadian Navy onto the world stage was designed by Smith's Dock Co. Ltd. of the UK in 1939, and it was based on the company's recent whale catcher, Southern Pride. A few modifications were made to the hull, superstructure, internal layout, communications equipment and accommodation to produce what was termed an auxiliary 'patrol vessel.'

Winston Churchill, First Lord of the Admiralty when World War II broke out, wanted to give the little ships names rather than numbers, and thought it would be good public relations to report that on of Hitler's sea wolves (U-boats) had been destroyed by a vessel named for a flower, like His Majesty's Ship Buttercup. So the Royal Navy dubbed the new ships 'Flower-class corvettes' and gave them all names like Hibiscus and Poppy. The first British corvettes were ordered in July 1939, the same month that plans for the vessels arrived in Canada.

The Canadian corvette HMCS *Penetang* was reactivated after her WW2 service and converted to a Prestonian-class frigate in 1953.

Bedford Basin is the largest part of Halifax harbour and served as the assmbly point for the Allied Trans-Atlantic convoys in the Second World War.

right: A still from the 1943 Universal movie *Corvette K225* which starred Randolf Scott, Ella Raines, Barry Fitzgerald and Noah Beery Jr.; below: Manning a depth-charge launcher; at bottom: A Hurricane "catafighter" on its catapult; bottom right: The Canadian Fleet minesweeper HMCS *Clayoquot*, J174.

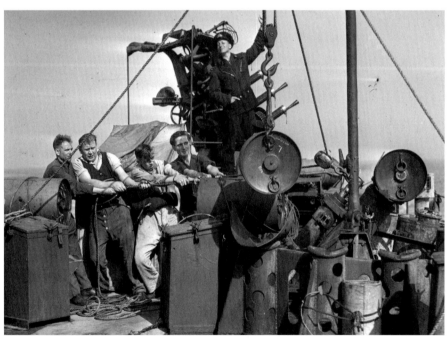

below: Captain Donald Macintyre, RN, captured Germany's greatest U-boat ace, Korvettenkapitán Otto Kretschmer.

left and above: Views of Second World War British and Canadian convoy escort vessels.

below: Firing a Mk II depth-charge thrower from the Royal Canadian Flower-class corvette HMCS *Pictou*.

. . . he wanted to prove he could attack by night on the surface and carry out his personal principle of 'one torpedo, one ship.' Fans of torpedoes were, in his opinion, a waste of equipment and effort and allowed a U-boat com-mander to attack from a position of comparative safety in the hope of hitting something, instead of

taking carefully calculated risks and by precision firing making every torpedo count. It was from this time that he became the first commander to attack convoys only by night and always on the surface. This attack was to set the pattern. At this stage of the war no other commanders followed Kretschmer's technique, considering it too dangerous, yet it was this method that led him to outstrip his colleagues in sinkings.

—from *The Golden Horseshoe* by Terence Robertson

above and overleaf: German U-boat crewmen
rescued by crews of U.S. Coast vessels.

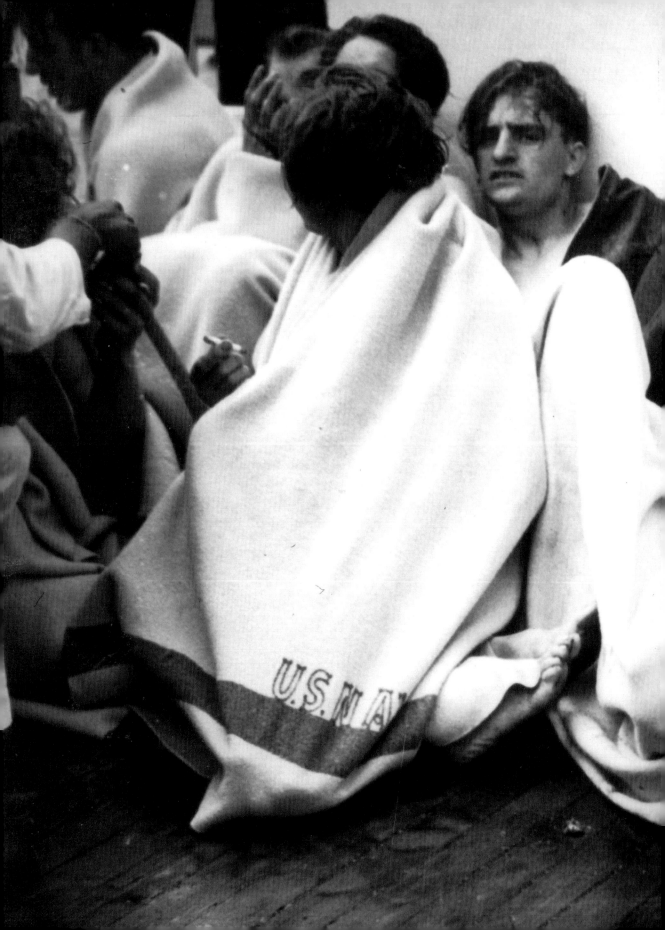

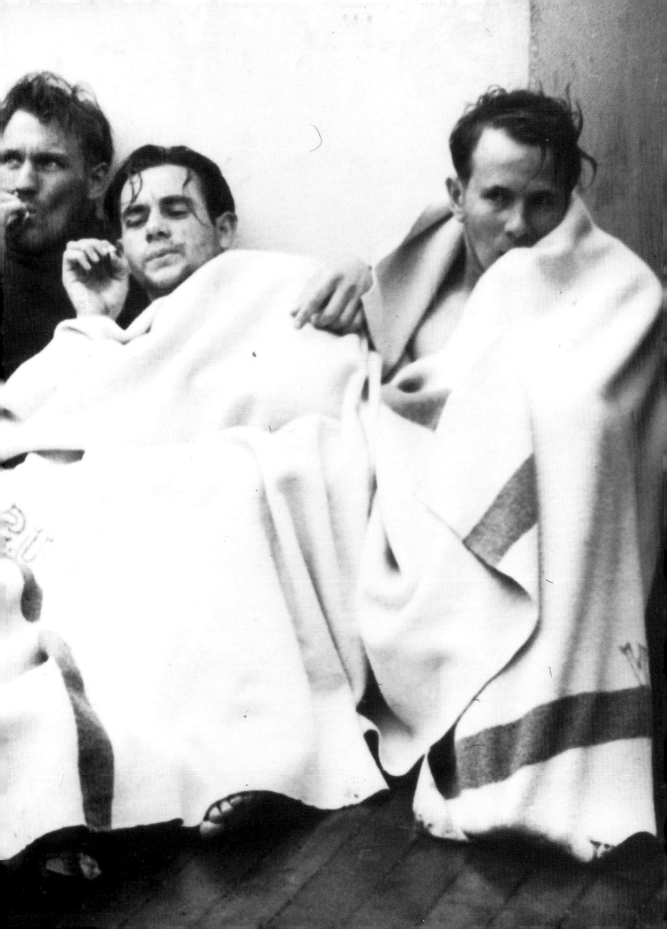

left: Crewmen of the submarine *U-858*, having become prison-ers-of-war; below: Prisoners from the crew of *U-175* being marched ashore by British Marines at Gourock, Scotland; right: A U-boat crew member captured by a U.S. Coast Guard crew.

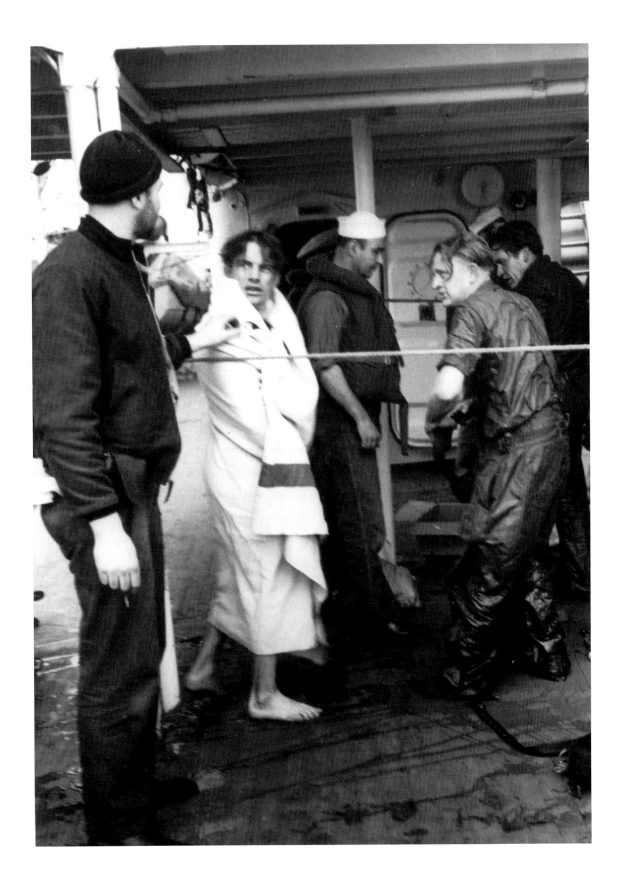

Run To The Red Star

Of all the routes sailed by the Allied merchant fleets in World War Two, the northeast route to Russia will surely be remembered as the one which posed the greatest challenge to the seaworthiness of ships and the hardihood of men. There were other routes as hazardous, but none which combined the dangers like the Russian run. It was a route on which the merchant ships and their escorts were under threat of attack by the enemy all the way from the hour of their departure until the hour of their return. From their bases on the north Norwegian coast, the Luftwaffe commanded much of the route with Ju 87B Stuka dive-bombers, He 111 torpedo-bombers, Ju 88 light bombers, and the four-engined reconnaissance Focke-Wulf Condors. Packs of U-boats, some withdrawn from the Atlantic, patrolled the Barents and Norwegian Seas; and at any time, one of the German big ships might emerge from the fiord where she lurked—the 43,000 ton battleship *Admiral von Tirpitz* with her formidable armament, the cruiser *Admiral Hipper*, and the fast pocket battleships *Admiral Scheer* and *Lützow*, all with their attendant escorts of destroyers.

For seamen who were unaccustomed to the nature of the Arctic, there was the striking contrast between seasons: the perpetual daylight hours of summer and the ferocious weather and long nights of winter, when dawn and twilight were divided by an hour and when an unseen "growler", drifting from the icepack, could tear a hole in a ship below the waterline. "In the ice," said one convoy Commodore, "it's better to be loaded than light. When you're light, the rudder and propellers may strike ice and be damaged; loaded, they're below it, and they're safe."

The winter scene was spectacular: the forecastles, bridges, hoists, davits, lifeboats and deck cargoes thick with milk-white ice, the sea-spray freezing where it struck. There was beauty, also, on the Arctic journey with the eerie, multi-coloured splendour of Aurora Borealis, shimmering and flashing in the polar sky.

In the early summer of 1941, Hitler decided that his duplicitous non-aggression pact with Stalin had run its course, and that the time had come to put their relations on a more realistic footing. He launched Operation Barbarossa on 22 June, and over 160 German divisions, strongly supported by the Luftwaffe, attacked on a 500-mile front. The British Empire and the Union of Soviet Socialist Republics were allies from that moment on. No matter that Stalin had taken cynical advantage of the British and French preoccupation with the western front to sieze the eastern part of Poland and annex the Baltic States, no matter that Russia had supplied Germany with oil and grain up to the very eve of Barbarossa—all that was in the past. Hitler had contrived by a single cataclysmic act to bring about an alliance, uneasy as it might sometimes prove to be, between Moscow and London, between the philosophically incompatible forces of Marxism and capitalism.

In his subsequent history of the war, Winston Churchill told a tale, possibly apocryphal, about a Royal Marine who, at that time, was being shown the sights of Moscow by a Russian guide. "This is the Eden Hotel," said the guide, "formerly the Ribbontrop Hotel. And here is Churchill Street, formerly Hitler Street, and this is Beaverbrook Station, formerly Goering Station. Will you have a cigarette, comrade?" The marine accepted. "Thank you, comrade, formerly bastard."

The outcome was that, in the Anglo-Soviet Trade Agreement of August 1941, Britain grant-ed Russia a five-year credit of £10,000,000 at 3.5% interest, and the first convoy of military aid sailed from Loch Ewe in Scotland, assembled at Hvalfiordur, an inlet on the west coast of Iceland, which had been occupied by the British and Canadians in May 1940 to pre-empt an invasion by the Germans. Hvalfiordur means "fiord of the whale", but was more often thought of by all who passed that way as "that God-forsaken place". On 21 August 1941, the first convoy sailed from Britain for Archangel on the river Dvina (which was ice-free in the summer months). It comprised six elderly tramps carrying wool, tin and rubber, with fifteen Hurricane fighters packed into their holds, and was escorted by three destroyers, three minesweepers (well-armed vessels and as fast as a corvette), and three anti-submarine trawlers. Interference by German surface ships was discouraged by a Home Fleet cover force as far as Bear Island, and the convoy was closely followed by the veteran aircraft carrier HMS *Argus*, with a strong RAF contingent and twenty-four Hurricanes, which later flew off her flight deck and landed safely on the Russian airfield at Vaenga in the Kola Inlet.

The first convoy was code-named Operation Dervish, while subsequent outbound con-voys were coded PQ (after the initials of Commander Peter Quellyn Russell, an Admiralty planner), and homebound convoys were logically QP. In January 1942, when the effect of the Japanese air assault on Pearl Harbor was to bring Britain a truer and more welcome ally, President Roosevelt and Prime Minister Churchill, meeting in Washington, agreed that they must first defeat Germany before turning on Japan, and that, as a corollary, they must at all costs "keep the Russians in the war". It meant that America would join Britain in providing Marshal Stalin's forces with a growing volume of military supplies.

Originally, the Anglo-Soviet Agreement had been signed on the basis that the supplies would be loaded onto Russian freighters at British, and later, at American ports, but few such ships materialised, and it transpired that the Soviet Union neither had, nor would ever have, enough to undertake the task. The whole burden of the Russian convoys was to fall on the hard-pressed British Board of Admiralty and, in particular, on Admiral Jack Tovey, C-in-C, Home Fleet. He knew that the escorts had to come from the resources of Western Approaches Command, where they were manifestly needed. He did not like that, nor did he care for the commitment, least of all in summer, and he said so, but Churchill was the boss, and the job had to be done.

Beginning in July, a monthly quota of at least 400 tanks and 300 combat aircraft were allo-cated to the Russians, and the convoys went on sailing, every ten or fourteen days, until the war was won. Towards the end, it entailed the assignment of warships to merchantmen on a ratio of one to one, but the convoys still went on. The total cost of the equipment carried to Russia by ships registered in Britain was $428,000,000.

When the merchant seamen stepped ashore in Murmansk, the conditions that they met were, as was to be expected, exceptionally bleak—the enemy, after all, was only thirty miles away. Almost every building on the miles of waterfront had been damaged or destroyed by Luftwaffe bombers. The citizens seldom showed much sign of friendliness, and, with a short-age of cranes, transportation and skilled labour, unloading cargoes took an age, while a queue of ships lay at anchor in Vaenga Bay, waiting for their turn. Ironically, the port, whose name in the local language meant "the end of the earth", had been built with British aid in 1915 at

overleaf *Convoy To Russia* by Charles Pears; above: The engine room of a Type VII U-boat.

the behest of the Tsar.

On 20 March 1942, convoy PQ13, made up of nineteen ships, British, American, Panamanian and Polish, assembled off Iceland and set course for Murmansk. Covering the first stage of the convoy's passage, and hoping to lure the German big ships out of the Norwegian fiords into battle, were two British battleships, a carrier, three cruisers and eleven destroyers, while the convoy's close escort consisted of the cruiser HMS *Trinidad*, in which the escort commander, Rear-Admiral Bonham-Carter, flew his flag, two destroyers and three ex-Norwegian whalers earmarked as reinforcements for the Russian Navy's minesweeper fleet. Convoy QP9, meanwhile, also well-escorted, was half-way along its homeward route.

The two-way operation had been carefully planned, but few plans survive their first contact with the enemy, particularly in Arctic weather. Convoy QP9 ran into a severe storm on 24 March, but managed to keep formation and continue west, while PQ13 had a harder time of it. In a strong southwesterly gale, mountainous seas and heavy snow, station-keeping was almost impossible, as was communication with the convoy Commodore in the *River Afton*. The lookouts were blinded and numbed by the cold, and the convoy had become, not an integrated unit, but merely a collection of individual ships proceeding approximately east. Furthermore, whenever there was a break in the cloud cover, Ju 88s based at Banak and Petsamo took the opportunity to make a series of attacks. On HMS *Trinidad*, Captain Sanders broke his radio silence (and his orders) to acquaint the Admiralty, Admiral Tovey and the

Closing the U-boat hatch in preparation to dive.   The ice-encrusted conning tower of a Type VII.

Senior British Naval Officer North Russia with the deteriorating situation.

On 27 March, when PQ13 should have made a rendezvous south of Bear Island, only seven vessels were in the vicinity, and Trinidad, with a destroyer, set about the task of rounding up the rest. The *River Afton*, meanwhile, had been isolated and, having evaded the attack of a surfaced U-boat, all the Commodore could do was to continue on his course to Murmansk on his own (sadly, the *River Afton*, which had first sailed on the Russian run from Iceland with PQ1 on 28 September 1941, did not survive the later horrors of PQ17).

That night, the *Induna* was endeavouring to tow the armed trawler HMS *Silja*, which was almost out of fuel, through the ice, when she was torpedoed. Her lifeboats were crowded, and injured men lay freezing while the remainder tried to bale. In one boat, fourteen men died in the next three days, and their bodies were dropped overboard, before a Soviet minesweeper arrived to save sixteen survivors. Of the ten men alive in the other lifeboats, two died later in a Murmansk hospital.

Three German destroyers of the Eighth Flotilla, *Z24, Z25* and *Z26,* now sailed out from Kirkenes, between North Cape and Murmansk, to intercept the convoy, and soon found the survivors of the 7,000-ton *Empire Ranger*, which had been sunk by bombing, freezing in their lifeboats. Another lifeboat, containing thirty-eight men, had floated for six days in appalling weather before being sighted from a Russian tug. Only the bosun and a fourteen-year-old cabin boy, both badly frost-bitten, had survived, and the bosun's legs and arms had to be am-

For the safety of the boat and and her crew, and the success of their mission, lookouts were always on duty when a U-boat was on the surface; above centre: The badge of the Ubootwaffe.

putated to save the poor man's life.

Trinidad, still hunting up the remaining stragglers, sighted the destroyer *Z26*, and there followed an inconclusive exchange of shots. It was *Trinidad*'s bad luck that the special low-temperature oil in her torpedo tubes had frozen, and when that was cleared and a torpedo was launched, it had a gyro malfunction. Turning back whence it came, the rogue torpedo blew a hole in the cruiser's port side, rupturing an oil tank and flooding the forward boiler room. The enemy destroyers, however, now turned back to the southwest, hotly pursued by the destroyers *Fury* and *Eclipse*, which caught *Z26* and sank her with gunfire. *Trinidad* eventually reached the Kola Inlet with Russian tugs in close attendance, but not required to give assistance. Five merchant ships, totalling 30,000 tons, had been lost from the complement of PQ13. Once ashore in Murmansk, the survivors were subjected to heavy air attack every day and night for the next three weeks.

HMS *Edinburgh*, now Bonham-Carter's flagship, was lying off Vaenga in the Kola Inlet on 27 April 1942, preparing to escort QP11 on the homeward route, when a lighter came alongside from which, under the eyes of Soviet soldiers and Royal Marines, a number of heavy boxes were loaded on board. It was not ammunition, however, which went below into the cruiser's magazine, but five tons of bullion for the United States Treasury—payment for American war supplies.

The thirteen-ship convoy sailed the next day, and was soon sighted by a pack of U-boats. The attacks began on the 30th, and *Edinburgh*, steaming ahead of the merchant ships, was hit by two torpedoes which destroyed her stern, her rudder and her two inner screws. She could be of no help to the convoy in that condition, and with four destroyers and two minesweepers for protection, Captain Faulkner turned back to Murmansk, while QP11, brilliantly defended by the remaining two destroyers and four corvettes, continued westward through the ice.

Next day, *Edinburgh* was well down by the stern, her list was steeper and she could not be steered. More U-boat attacks were beaten off, and a tow was attempted by HMS *Foresight*, but when three German destroyers appeared, Bonham-Carter ordered the line to be cast off. By now, the cruiser was swinging round in circles, but she and her destroyers continued to maintain a fierce rate of fire. Then, she was hit twice more by torpedoes, and the Rear-Admiral told Faulkner to give the order to abandon. Two minesweepers, HMS *Harrier* and *Gossamer*, came alongside to take off her crew, and Bonham-Carter hoisted his flag in *Harrier*. As he and Faulkner gazed at the slowly settling cruiser, the Captain had a sudden thought. In quieter moments, he and the Rear-Admiral had amused themselves by playing backgammon, and Faulkner was the better player. "I'm going back on board for a moment," he said. "What the devil for? asked Bonham-Carter. "For the tally," said Faulkner, "you owe me thirty pounds!" The other shook his head: "I'm afraid the tally goes down with the ship, and with the Russian gold."

Bonham-Carter arrived in Murmansk to find HMS *Trinidad*, with her plates patch-welded, braced with lengths of rail track "borrowed" from the Russians by a naval raiding party, but with only her after boiler room capable of providing steam for the turbines. Nevertheless, his flag was hoisted and *Trinidad* set out from Murmansk with four destroyers to catch up with QP11. In the Barents Sea the merchantmen and warships came under heavy air attack, and, on 15 May a Ju 88 hit *Trinidad* with a cluster of four bombs. Down by the bow, and listing to starboard, the cruiser fought on, and her gunners had the savage satisfaction of destroying her attacker, but her fuel tanks were ablaze, the fire was spreading and Captain Davies was obliged to give the order to abandon ship. An Engineer Lieutenant insisted on going below to ensure that all of the stokers had emerged, and he did not return. His award of the Albert Medal was posthumous. HMS *Foresight* manoeuvred carefully alongside to take off her surviving crew and passengers—the injured seamen of PQ13—and the HMS *Matchless* administered the coup de grace with a couple of torpedoes.

Since Bonham-Carter sailed with PQ14 as escort commander, five warships had gone down under him, of which *Trinidad* was the last. A well-liked officer, if unlucky at backgammon and in his choice of flagships, it was he who was perceptively to write: "We in the navy are paid to do this sort of job, but it is beginning to ask to much of the men in the Merchant Navy. We may be able to avoid bombs and torpedoes with our speed. A six or eight-knot ship has not this advantage."

On 16 June 1942, one of PQ13's survivors, the *Empire Starlight*, sank in the shallow water of the Kola Inlet. Almost every day, from 4 April, when she anchored off Murmansk, until she was finally unloaded and abandoned, the German bombers seemed to seek her out for particular attention. Her master, Captain Stein, could have been forgiven for believing that the Luftwaffe was pursuing a personal vendetta against him and his Chinese crew. After persistent and almost daily bombings in mid-April, during which her gunners accounted for three of her attackers, she was only kept afloat by the heroic efforts of Russian divers and her crew. The bombing was relentlessly pursued throughout the month of May, when she was loaded with pit-props and timber for the journey back to England, and if she was not the most bombed vessel in the merchant fleet, she must have run the record holder very close. The award of OBEs to her Captain and Chief Engineer cannot be regarded as being over-generous, but it is good to know that, after the war, the *Empire Starlight* was raised, refitted, and resumed her trade.

The Soviet Admiral Golovko, commanding Russia's Northern Fleet, came to enjoy a love-hate relationship with the Royal Navy, and indeed the U.S. Navy, whose members, and especially the officers, he tended to regard as capitalist imperialists—the sort of men who would have been on the Tsar's side in the revolution of 1917. This view was shared by many Soviet officials. Golovko deplored the way a British naval escort would sink a stricken merchant ship with gunfire, having taken off her crew, rather than risk her cargo falling to the enemy. He took the view that such action should only be taken when it was absolutely certain that salvage was impossible.

Meanwhile, the Red Army had counter-attacked with enormous courage, and there had been appalling losses on both sides. "We have seriously underestimated the Russians," confided General Heinz Guderian, pioneer and main protagonist of German tank warfare. There was a stalemate for a while until, in the summer of 1942, Hitler took personal command, and soon his armies in Russia were moving east again, killing and capturing thousands of prisoners. Marshal Timoshenko's Army Group was forced back to the River Don and ordered to defend Stalingrad to the last man. It is ironic that, at a time when Stalin was urging the Allies to

"open a second front in Europe", battalions of Red Army POWs were, albeit unwillingly, helping the German Todt construction gangs to strengthen the Atlantic Wall of the Führer's Fortress Europe.

Gradually, the Russian port facilities improved, due largely to the efforts of Royal Navy working parties, joined by U.S. Navy men. Often under air attack, they worked under the direction of the Senior British Naval Officer North Russia, a Rear-Admiral, whose tasks included obtaining assistance for the convoys from Russian destroyers, minesweepers and ice-breakers, of organising anchorage and berthing for the merchantmen, and of their replenishment with fuel, water, stores, and ammunition for the homeward run. These tasks were never easy, and they also embraced the even more demanding one of liaison with the hard-nosed Admiral Golovko. For the majority of visitors, contact with the Russians was largely through interpreters, many of whom were women, few of whom were helpful, and most of whom were either members of, or closely connected with, Russia's secret police force, the NKVD.

Relations between the Royal and Merchant Navies were always rather tenuous, and the tensions of the Arctic convoys almost brought them to the breaking point. Rightly or wrongly, by mid-summer 1942, some merchant seamen were beginning to suspect that, as well as helping "Uncle Joe", there was another reason for the Russian run, and that was to tempt the German big ships out onto the high seas, where they might come within the range of the British Home Fleet's guns. "Their Lordships in London don't give a toss for us," was the general tenor of this feeling, "nor for the Russkies either, come to that."

Rear-Admiral Hamilton, the commander of PQ17's cruiser escort wrote in his operation order: "The primary object is to get PQ17 to Russia, but an object only slightly subsidiary is to provide an opportunity for the enemy's heavy ships to be brought to action." It was, after all, inherent in a navy man that he should regard the sinking of the *Tirpitz*, or of any German battleship, as a more important matter, in the wider context of the war at sea, than the protection of freighters taking arms to Russia. So the seamen's suspicions may not have been entirely without foundation.

Among the supplies reaching Russia by the northern route (and these were in addition to the greater quantities which came through the Persian Gulf and thence by rail from Basra to the Caspian), were 7,400 aircraft, including 3,000 from America, 5,200 tanks (1,390 from Canada), 5,000 anti-tank and anti-aircraft guns, 4,000 rifles and machine-guns, 1,800 radar sets, 4,000 radios, 2,000 sets of telephone equipment, fourteen minesweepers, nine motor torpedo boats and four submarines. There can be little doubt that this materiel, plus ammunition and torpedoes, medical supplies and hospital equipment, food and industrial plant, tin, wool and rubber, were of crucial help to Stalin's armies. These supplies enabled the Russians to withstand the German invasion, eventually to repel it, to win the great tank battle on the plains of Kursk in 1943, and to move onto the offensive to such good effect that they not only drove the Wehrmacht back, but continued moving west until they reached the German capital before the Western Allies.

Between August 1941 and May 1945, forty convoys, each comprising roughly twenty merchant ships, made the voyage to Russia; ten per cent of the ships involved were sunk by the enemy en route, while act of God or accident accounted for the loss of nineteen more. The ships which carried the equipment from America, and those which took it on to Russia, sailed under many different flags, and from 1942 onwards the U.S. Navy often assisted in escorting them. The responsibility, however, of mounting the convoys, and seeing them through the 2,000 miles or more from Iceland, at longitude 20 degrees west, to Murmansk or Archangel, at 33 or 42 degrees east, fell to the Royal Navy.

The threat from the enemy—surface warships, U-boats or aircraft—had to be accepted by every man who sailed the seas in wartime, and the brutal cold and ever-present ice that made the Russian run a peculiarly horrible experience. It was small comfort to the Allied seamen to know, as they crept between North Cape and Bear Island, and through the Barents Sea, trying to maintain some sort of formation, that conditions in the Arctic Circle were as hostile to the Kriegsmarine as to the navies of the Allies.

Few merchant seamen particularly enjoyed the time they had to spend on Russian soil, where they often found suspicion, waste, and ingratitude. To move about in town was to run the gauntlet of unfriendly guards at every gate and doorway, who could be relied on to find some discrepancy in any pass or ID papers. Mail was interferred with or delayed, and any Soviet official, whether male or female, who showed signs of a friendly disposition, would soon mysteriously disappear. It angered the seamen to see lines of new Hurricanes, which had been brought to Russia at great risk, standing idle and uncovered, open to the elements, because the Russians were too lazy, or too inefficient, to repair some minor damage caused on landing or unloading.

The survivors of that most ill-used of convoys, PQ17, in their time ashore in Archangel, subsisted on a diet of black bread, barley and grass soup, and, with the local medical resources overwhelmed by the battle casualties from the front line barely thirty miles away, the treatment for their injured was primitive at best. "There was only one redeeming feature," said a stoker, "the vodka was cheap."

Not all the defects, however, were on the Russian side. The charge was laid at Murmansk (and seized upon by Stalin), that cargoes loaded in Britain, as opposed to in America, were often found to have been damaged en route, arguably due to the British method of putting the heaviest items low in a ship which, the Russians claimed, tended to make the vessel laterally unstable and, as she rolled, to cause the lashing wires to penetrate the packaging and lacerate the goods.

There were a number of occasions when the heavy units of the opposing navies sailed in all their pomp across great stretches of the northern seas, the one under orders to destroy a convoy but, on no account, to get into a battle; the other directed to engage the enemy if possible, but, on the other hand, to protect the convoy. Signals flashed through the ether from London and Berlin: Ultra decryptions were suggesting one thing, while B-dienst intercepts indicated another, and the big ships altered course accordingly. Consequently, it was only the aircrew, flying off the carriers or launched from the battleships, who got to fire a shot in anger.

The voyage of convoy PQ17 in June 1942, was a disaster. Most of the escort was withdrawn by the Admiralty in London to meet what turned out to be a non-existent threat from the *Tirpitz*, leaving the merchantmen to struggle on to Archangel, virtually undefended. It was also, unhappily, the first combined Anglo-American naval operation. Of the thirty-five merchant ships which set out from Iceland, eight were sunk by aircraft, and eight by U-boats, which also finished off another eight already damaged by the aircraft. This slaughter was achieved at a cost to the enemy of six bomber aircraft. 153 merchant seamen and one Royal Navy man were killed, and it was probably those figures which, more than any other, gave rise to the feelings of resentment on the one side and of shame upon the other. The feelings within the Merchant Navy led to condemnation and recriminations, stated or unstated, which have cast a long, dark shadow down the years. When at last the survivors arrived in Glasgow with the inbound QP14, they were addressed by the Ministry of War Transport's Under-Secretary of State, who found it in himself to say of their ordeal that "whatever the cost, it was worth it", before he was shouted down.

Meanwhile a Soviet Navy Captain on Golovko's staff had declaimed at a post-convoy conference: "It is not enough; we want more tanks, more planes . . ." Marshal Stalin would have approved of that. In due course, though, four of the merchant masters were awarded the Distinguished Service Order, the first of their service to be so decorated. More significantly, in the context of the war, the Arctic convoys were suspended for the next two months of constant daylight, and when PQ18 sailed from Loch Ewe on 2 September 1942, it was with a Home Fleet cover force, its own light carrier carrying three Swordfish and six Sea Hurricanes of the Fleet Air Arm, and two destroyer squadrons—one for close escort and one to range freely, giving battle wherever it was offered. Despite this high level of support, thirteen of the forty-eight-ship convoy were sunk, ten by torpedo-bombers, but the gallant, steadfast conduct of the Royal Navy escort did much to restore the respect of the American Merchant Marine, if not entirely of the British Merchant Navy.

During those two months, when only half-a-dozen comparatively fast single ships made the Russian run, Admiral Tovey did his best to provide succeeding convoys, both PQ and QP, with strong, fighting escorts, adequately supported by fleet oilers, through the most dangerous sectors of their routes. The additional destroyers could only come from the Western Approaches Command but, as Dönitz was withdrawing U-boats from his Bay of Biscay bases to patrol the Barents Sea, a sort of balance was maintained in the Atlantic. Despite continuous attacks throughout the war, the German bombers had few successes against the merchantmen in the Kola Inlet, and the reason may have been the prodigious, if sometimes ill-directed, anti-aircraft barrage thrown up by the Russians and from the ships themselves. In addition to the *Empire Starlight,* as has been recorded, only three merchantmen were sunk, while another two succombed to mines in Murmansk Roads.

One survivor of PQ18 was a 1st Mate, who reached the south island of Novaya Zemlya, alone in an open boat, and scrambled ashore to replenish his supply of fresh water. Glancing at the rocks below, he observed a flock of ducks and, with more hope than confidence, let down a length of rope with a running bowline on the end. One of the birds promptly inserted its head, and he continued angling until he had collected enough to live on roast duck (the resourceful fellow contrived to light a fire) for the remainder of his stay on the island.

The saga of the Russian convoys took a better turn in the autumn of 1944, when 159 ships made the voyage and not a one was lost. Overall, however, the Royal Navy had lost eighteen warships and almost 2,000 officers and men, while eighty-seven merchant ships had gone down with an average of a hundred men on each. For their part, the Germans had lost a battleship, three destroyers, thirty-two U-boats and as many aircraft. It had been a bitter and prolonged battle. With its surviving veterans, it rankles that the Merchant Navy's heroic contribution was never recognised by a campaign medal.

It was when he was presenting some Russian decorations to British officers and seamen who had made many voyages to Archangel or Murmansk, that Mr Ivan Maisky, the Soviet Ambassador to Britain, spoke of their missions in these terms: "They are a northern saga of heroism, bravery and endurance, and the price had to be paid. This saga will live forever, not only in the hearts of your people, but also in the hearts of the Soviet People, who rightly see in it one of the most striking expressions of collaboration between the Allied nations."

Though displaying elan and gallantry, neither the Soviet navy nor its air force ever relieved the Home Fleet of any apprciable share of the responsibility for the defence of an Arctic convoy.
—from *The War at Sea* by S. Roskill

The Soviet Government had the impression that they were conferring a great favour on us by fighting in their own country for their own lives. The more they fought the heavier our debt became.
—Winston S. Churchill

Through icy, fog-bound seas, their flanks exposed to the dive-bombers, surface raiders and submarines moving out from the Nazi-held fiords of Norway the slow gray convoys moved—and kept moving. Nor was there sanctuary at their destination, for every hour on the hour,

Christmas at sea in a U-boat; right: The captain conducting the business of the boat.

it was said, the black-crossed planes of the Luftwaffe blasted heart-breaking delays in the grim business of unloading the ships in the ice-cluttered harbor of Murmansk. Yet the cargoes were delivered.

—from the post-war report by the American War Shipping Administration to President Harry S. Truman

The design for the Victory ship was completed in 1943 and the first ship was delivered in 1944. The Victory was turbine-powered with 8,500 horsepower and she cruised at fifteen knots. 414 of the Victory ships had been built by the end of the war, and an additional 117 were built after the war, some of which saw service in the Vietnam war.

Be sure your lifeboat is seaworthy. This may seem needless advice. Yet in the past, bottoms have come out of many lifeboats. One lifeboat of a United Nations freighter, torpedoed 200 miles from Bermuda, leaked so badly that for eleven days the men were unable to stop baling.

Every man should have a whistle made fast around his neck, so that if he is in the water, he can blow the whistle to draw attention. Life lights are manufactured for both jackets and life rings. With good visibility these lights will provide a possibility of attracting rescuers within a radius of at least four miles. Within the visibility range of shore, they offer a three-way chance of drawing attention—from land, sea and air.

If you are on watch, you should have your life suit, extra clothes, and abandon-ship pack-

age with you, so you will not have to lose time returning to your quarters. Do not take it for granted that all the equipment required by law is in your lifeboat. Norman Lee Sampson, the third assistant of a torpedoed freighter, reported that nine of his shipmates were trapped in a lifeboat with no oars. The boat drifted into a sea of blazing oil.
—from *How To Abandon Ship* by Phil Richards and John J. Banigan

It started with a single aircraft, possibly an old friend, a four-engined Focke-Wulf reconnaissance plane which closed the convoy from eastwards and then began to go round them in slow circles, well out of range of any gunfire they could put up. It had happened to them before, and there was little doubt of what the plane was doing—pin-pointing the convoy, shadowing it, noting exactly its course and speed, and then reporting back to some central authority, as well as tipping off any U-boats that might be nearby. The change this time lay in the fact that it was occurring so early in their voyage, and that, as they watched the plane circling and realized its mission, the sun was pouring down from a matchless sky on to a sea as smooth and as lovely as old glass, hardly disturbed at all by the company of ships that crossed it on their way southwards. Unfair to peace-loving convoys, they thought as they closed their ranks and trained their glasses on the slowly-circling messenger of prey: leave us alone on this painted ocean, let us slip by, no one will know . . .
—from *The Cruel Sea* by Nicholas Monsarrat

Rudy Radmanovich was a member of the U.S. Merchant Marine in World War Two. In the winter of 1944 he shipped out of New York as an oiler aboard the Liberty ship, SS *Stephen Leacock*. The ship was routed to Halifax where they picked up an escort for the north of England. In the Hebrides they joined another convoy which set course north through the Norwegian Sea, the Arctic Sea, and finally the White Sea north of Archangel. In navigating the North Cape, the convoy was caught between Nazi planes, submarines, mines, and surface warships. They went as close to the ice pack as they could, but were unable to evade the German attacks. Fourteen of the thirty-four merchant ships of Rudy's convoy managed to reach Russia. Twenty of the vessels were sunk in the ice-choked waters, and few of the crew members survived. Rudy served on in the Merchant Marine through the end of the war. He was awarded the Merchant Marine Combat Bar, the Atlantic, Mediterranean and Pacific War Zone medals, and the Merchant Marine Victory medal, as well as the Russian Medal of Commemoration for the Murmansk Convoy Survivors.

The *Schoharie* was berthed only a few streets from the Navy Yard and when we reboarded, her winches and booms were rolling cables in and out as cargo was hoisted aboard from the dock and lowered into the hatches for storage. Pallets of jerry cans filled with gasoline and crates of heavy duty ammo were being stored below. "Goddamn, we're not a tanker", yelled Lagola, the coxs'n. Nevertheless, the loading of the jerry cans and the ammunition continued for several days until finally the hatches were closed and secured with tarpaulin. Next came the deck cargo: locomotives, trucks, and huge wooden crates. The whole deck and hatches fore and aft, were packed solid with deck cargo. We wondered whether the ship would sail or sink under such a load. The locomotives were stencilled in white paint with lettering that didn't make sense: 0006095ARKHSU775698. Of course, this was the manufacturer's or

shipping agent's code. The next evening a dozen cartons were delivered to the Navy crew. They contained foul weather gear and athletic game equipment. The armed guard was well-equipped for the expected bitter cold of the Atlantic. We were issued cold weather, sea arctics, winter trousers (lined bibbed overalls), winter mittens, winter face masks and goggles, and heavy parka jackets, all in addition to the standard sou'wester rain hat, oilskin coat and trousers. There surely was no secret where we were headed and many guessed we were going to Murmansk, Russia. The scuttlebutt gang were always speculating on every rumor and hunch that occurred to them. And so the guessing game began. But for the time being, the only important thing was a last night of liberty. "Button Your Lip" and "Loose Lips Sink Ships" were the signs we read as we departed the ship. Fortunately, having a last night at home for the locals, and a good time in New York for the rest, probably did more to keep those lips closed. A few may have used "We're shipping out soon" to gain an extra kiss or more from a worried young lady. We don't know that anyone used the guessing game of our destination, except perhaps, "It's gonna be damn cold wherever we're going". But then, it was late September and at sea cold weather comes early. The mystery letters on the locomotives, we later realized, were Archangel Soviet Union, a rather obvious message to anyone who cared to know.
—Thom Hendrickson, DEMS signalman, U.S. Navy

I don't know how we ever slept on the Russian run. We had no heating whatever down below, other than a coal-burning stove on the messdeck, which we could only use when the chimney could be erected, sticking up on the foredeck, if the weather permitted. The condensation from our breath built up into ice six inches thick inside the messdecks, as of course, the deck above had no wood, only bare steel. We spent the whole time wrapped up in anything we could find. At sea I was supposed to sleep in the wheelhouse outside the wireless office, so as to be on immediate call. I wore a one-piece kapok zipped-up suit which had an oilskin outer cover for working on the upper deck. I had also obtained a pair of wooden-soled fisherman's boots in Iceland, which were very efficient and, over my shoulders, as I could not wear it any other way, a duffle coat. The night before our return, some of us were invited to attend a cinema show on board *Edinburgh*, and the Russian sentries posted on every gangway annoyed us with their insistence on seeing our identity cards every time we passed them. Of course, at that time we knew nothing of the millions in gold bars being loaded on the *Edinburgh* and soon to spend many years at the bottom of the Barents Sea. Our original escort group sailed on 28 April, with two Russian destroyers escorting QP11 and very quickly ice started to form all over the ship, the upper deck crew keeping themselves warm by chipping off ice from the guns and depth charge throwers. Within two days the *Edinburgh* had been torpedoed by *U-456*, but did not sink. However, she could only go around in circles. At this time six German destroyers moved in to finish off the *Edinburgh*, and our destroyers *Amazon*, *Bulldog*, *Forester* and *Foresight* took them on in a classic line gun battle, helped by *Edinburgh*'s guns. The leading German destroyer, the *Hermann Schoeman*, was blown out of the water, which discouraged the others, but by 1 May, *Edinburgh* had sunk with all the gold.
—Cyril Hatton, Leading Telegraphist, HMS *Snowflake*

Upwards of 7,500 RAF pilot candidates were sent to the
United States for flight training under the Arnold Scheme
between June 1941 and February 1943.

Early flying training in the UK was conducted in the de
Havilland DH82 Tiger Moth.

Of all the aid provided by America to Britain in the early years of World War Two, not the least important was the training of pilots. This piece of the Lend-Lease package stemmed from an offer by General Henry "Hap" Arnold, Commander of the U.S. Army Air Corps (as it was then), to the RAF, of a third of the places in his expanding training programme. It was a generous offer, which was gratefully accepted, and between June 1941 and February 1943, over 7,500 embryo RAF pilots crossed the Atlantic to take their places in the "Arnold Scheme", as it was called. Nearly 4,500 young hopefuls completed the training successfully and returned to Britain with their wings. Jack Currie was one of them.

"There were seven of us who had contrived to stay together through the vicissitudes of initial ground school at Stratford-on-Avon and air experience at Ansty, and we were still together on Monday, 5 January 1942, aboard the troopship *Wolfe* as she lay off Gourock in the Firth of Clyde.

"The Stratford group's accommodation was not the most salubrious to be found aboard the ship: it was on the mess deck, next to the galley, way back astern and just above the Plimsoll line. A cheerful seaman showed us how to sling our hammocks and, as cheefully, charged half a crown for the two bits of wood which held the ends apart. The resulting contraption didn't look comfortable, but it was—once you had mastered the knack of getting into it without doing a barrel roll. That night, I slept like a baby, while the ship stood silent on the softly lapping tide.

"Next day at noon, the *Wolfe* moved out into the Firth and steamed slowly south between the Isle of Arran and the Ayrshire coast. Featonby, one of our number, appeared at the deck rail. 'In the canteen,' he said, 'there's as many cigarettes and chocolates as you want. It's just like peacetime.' The coastline faded, the breeze began to penetrate our greatcoats and we went below to play pontoon until the call for 'lights out'. Fully dressed, and wearing a life-jacket (ship's orders were insistent about that), I slept well again. It seemed like a moment before the clatter of cutlery and the smell of bacon frying announced another day, and it took no longer to swing out of the hammock and take a place at table.

"To breakfast so, unshaven and unwashed, seemed decidedly raffish, if not downright degenerate—I would not have got away with it at home—but so limited were *Wolfe*'s facilities that anyone attempting their ablutions at that hour of the day did so at the risk of missing breakfast altogether. Featonby, predictably, contrived to rise early, and was as neat as a pin. For the rest of us, two or three days without a razor didn't make much difference to our chins.

"When the morning lifeboat drill was held, the ship was steaming southward in the Irish Sea; she passed St David's Head in the early afternoon and came to anchor in Milford Haven, among the mastheads that protruded through the surface of the sound. "It's a ship's graveyard," said Lawton with a shudder. 'I hope we don't stay here long.' 'They've been sunk on purpose, mate', said Burt, 'block ships, they are, to prevent the U-boats sneaking in.' He glanced westward down the sound. 'The convoy'll form up here, I reckon. Last port of call before the old Atlantic. Safety in numbers, mate, against the U-boats—and the bloody *Tirpitz*.' We stared at this new, nautically knowledgeable Burt. '*Tirpitz*?'

'Your Jerry pocket battleships—don't you know anything about the war at sea?'

'Actually', said Featonby, 'the *Tirpitz* is bottled up in the Baltic, and daren't come out.'

Don't you believe it, Ron. It might bust out at any minute and come belting across the

at top: North American AT-6 trainer aircraft used by the American and British trainees for advanced flying training; above: German ground crew decorating their aircraft with "kill" markings.

Control tower staff on an airfield in England.

Atlantic, looking for such as us. That's why we'll sail in a great convoy, see?'

"This forecast of a great marshalling of British seapower to our side proved optimistic. When the convoy formed, even Burt had to admit that a solitary frigate and another tatty troopship fell short of what he had in mind. Nevertheless, it was in this company that the *Wolfe* set course that afternoon. Next morning, she was in the North Atlantic and rolling on the greenies like an empty barrel. Johnson had been one of those affected by the motion of the tender as it crossed the gentle Clyde; now, he was quite brought down, and sat throughout the day, with others equally distressed, swathed in blankets on the windswept afterdeck, his long, comedian's face a greenish-yellow shade. Mustering for lifeboat drill, we called a hearty greeting, to which he responded with the sickliest of grins.

"That afternoon, in what had been the First Class dining room before the *Wolfe* became a troopship, as many of the draft as could be crowded in were treated to a talk by a famous fighter pilot who, on a rest from operations, was bound for a lecture tour in the USA. Squadron Leader Gwilliam was physically slight, with fair, wavy hair a little longer than the norm and a youthful appearance, except for the network of lines around his eyes. He wore his tunic with the top button unfastened, in the fighter pilot's fashion, a row of medals and a pair of tennis shoes, for which he apologised—he had left a burning Spitfire just too late to save his toes. His talk, from what I heard of it (he spoke very quietly), was about the way the U.S. Army Air Corps trained their pilots. Many of us would have liked to have heard a word about his combat experience but, such were the inhibitions of the day, the obligatory reticence which made the slightest hint of 'line-shooting' utterly taboo, that no-one asked the hero to say a word about himself.

"In the afternoon of 10 January, Burt announced that a gale was blowing up. The *Wolfe* must have heard him, because she started behaving more eccentrically, adding pitching and tossing to the rolling and yawing we had come to know, if not to love. The path through the water was that of a corkscrew, and the group of the unwell on the afterdeck swelled by the minute. Withers, wearing a Balaclava helmet that made his head look like a turnip in a badly-holed sock, brought news of our sister ship. 'Apparently', he said, 'the electric steering gear's broken down. They've got eight men at the wheel and they still can't hold her on course.

"The prow climbed high into the lurid sky, with foam-flecked fountains spraying the decks, and paused as though uncertain of which way to go, swerved and plunged into a trough between two towering ridges in the roaring seascape. That night, swinging in the hammock, I heard sounds from the galley of the breaking of crockery, the clanging of pots and the slithering of pans—as though a gang of poltergiests were holding a convention. Breakfast next morning wasn't up to par, but the cooks produced a Sunday lunch—turkey and Christmas pudding—of which my mother would have approved. The howl of the gale and the tang of the spray were appetite enhancing and I approached every meal with a keenness only briefly blunted when an ill-fitting porthole cover allowed a stream of salty water to splash across the table.

"On Monday, although the *Wolfe*'s speed had been reduced to help her keep station, our sister ship was nowhere to be seen. She was somewhere far astern, and the frigate with her. McLeod scanned the horizon and the approaching snowstorm. 'This is jolly good', he said, 'all alone in the middle of the ocean. Where's the Navy gone?'

'You might well ask', said Withers. 'This area's absolutely thick with U-boats.'

Featonby sniffed, 'How on earth do you know? You haven't the faintest idea where we are.'

'I've been working it out, mate, and we're bang in the middle of their killing ground.' Excitedly, he pointed at the heaving greyness on the starboard beam. 'Look there, for Christ's sake! Isn't that a torpedo coming straight at us?' Walker cast a quick glance to his right. 'Shut your head, you panicky wee bugger', he said, 'or I'll throw you overboard. I'm away below for a game of pontoon.'

"We played the game by the hour, for a penny a card. That, and ship's duties, were all there was to do. There were so many of us to share out the duties—fatigues, security guard or crewing the Bofors gun—that the chances were against being on the roster more than once. When my turn came around it was fatigues—humping barrels in the canteen—which wasn't quite so boring as guarding nameless stores against an unknown predator, and a lot less chilling than manning the gun. Withers and I, co-humpers, listened to the rhythmic pounding—like a pneumatic drill working in slow time—as the gunners fired their practice rounds out there in the cold, and agreed that fatigues were not too bad after all.

In addition to RAF personnel training in the U.S., Royal Navy flying trainees were sent there under the Towers Scheme organised by Rear Admiral John H. Towers who had been the third licensed American naval aviator.

"Next day the weather was so hostile—'She's shipping the greenies,' Burt remarked—that only the duty gun crew were allowed on deck. Down below, the purser changed our sterling into dollars. 'I don't call this money,' said McLeod, fingering a not. 'We play Monopoly with stuff like this at home.'

"With nightfall came the sound of heavy gunfire, booming in the distance to the north. No-one told us what it meant—perhaps nobody knew—and it had been forgotten by the time the craggy coast of Nova Scotia appeared on the horizon with the dawn. The *Wolfe* dropped her anchor in Halifax harbour after fourteen days at sea, in the stinging cold of the late afternoon. Its brilliance was fading into twilight as we prepared to disembark.

"There was a moment, standing on deck with collar buttoned up and hands deep in pockets, while the shore-lights shone serenely and shimmered on the water, when it truly reached me that embattled, blacked-out Britain was 2,000 miles away, and that beyond the starlit harbour lay another world. I shuffled down the gangway, with Walker ahead of me, Featonby behind. On the far side of the snow-covered pier, hissing patiently, stood the train that was to take the draft to Moncton in New Brunswick. I stepped across the threshold into North

Arnold Scheme trainees returned to the UK to fly aircraft such as the Handley Page Halifax bomber. Jack Currie flew a tour of duty in Lancasters, instructed in Halifaxes and flew Mosquitos as a member of the elite Pathfinder Force; right: The pilot of a German Stuka dive-bomber.

America, slipped on a patch of ice and landed on my back.

"On 1 October 1942, with wings on my tunic, a sergeants chevrons on my sleeve, and 250 flying hours in my log-book, I was standing on the pier at Halifax again. This time, the passage was to take six days, and our ship, the *Stirling Castle*, was sailing in the sort of armada Percy Burt had dreamed of ten months ago at Milford Haven. And it wasn't only the size of the convoy, or its speed, which made the voyage so different from the earlier experience in HMT *Wolfe*. Then, if the draft, as aircrew under training, had gone to the bottom of the Atlantic, only our nearest and dearest would have cared; now, we could fly, and the squadrons needed us. Britain had invested a lot in our training, and was protecting her investment.

"No-one slung a hammock aboard the *Stirling Castle*, and someone else did the chores. We slept in bunks and dined in state—as though in a West End restaurant afloat. There was air protection, too.

The long, green sweep of Ireland's coastline looked peaceful and serene in the October sun, as though untouched by war, and it took the sight of Liverpool's disfigurement and Birkenhead's scars to tell us we were home. Everyone on deck was rather quiet as the *Stirling Castle* steamed up the Mersey—quiet, but content. I, for one, had seldom felt so happy. I didn't even fret when I discovered on the quay, that some light-fingered character had known exactly where to find those little presents for the family, wrapped and ready in a kit bag in the hold. That sort of mishap was just a part of coming home."

Clematis, a Flower-class corvette built by Charles Hill of Bristol, sailed down the Avon in the

late summer of 1940 under the command of a fine seaman and distinguished R.N.R. Commander, York McLeod Cleeves. She soon knew the hazards of the Atlantic. On her second convoy thirty-seven out of fifty-two ships were lost. She had towed a merchant ship— the SS *Ardoni*—back to Bristol waters and survived being the sitting target they both were. It was a good example of her Captain's seamanship qualities. It also earned salvage money for the ship's company. Shortly before Christmas 1940 she was one of the escorts of WS5A, a large troop convoy bound for South Africa. In addition to three other corvettes, there were three cruisers—*Bonaventure*, *Dunedin* and *Berwick*—as well as the aircraft carriers *Furious* and *Argus* loaded with aircraft for Africa. It was a considerable target. On Christmas day, *Clematis* was on the starboard bow of the convoy with a merchant ship—the *Empire Trooper*—which had strayed off her correct station in the convoy. At 0725 the officer of the watch and the yeoman of signals saw flashes on their starboard bow. They thought it was lightning until, to their alarm, shells started to drop round them. They then saw what they described as a large battleship some four miles off. The alarm bells were rung. The Captain immediately ordered full steam, altered course towards the enemy and ordered the gunners to open fire. At the same time he ordered a signal to be sent to the Admiralty which he realised would be picked up by the other naval ships in the convoy: 'Am engaging unknown enemy battleship' and gave our position. It was in fact the *Hipper*, but at that time was thought to be the *Admiral Scheer*. Miraculously, *Clematis* was not hit. The engine room were ordered to make smoke to shield the convoy while *Clematis* continued to fire her four-inch gun. Fortunately for *Clematis* and her ship's company, the cruisers and particularly *Berwick*, had by then picked up the signal

and had come round from the port side of the convoy. *Berwick*, in particular, opened fire and, although no match for the *Hipper*, persuaded her to withdraw. History in German records shows, *Hipper* did not wish to become involved in a battle early in her cruise. *Clematis* survived and so did *Empire Trooper* in spite of being hit. *Berwick* also suffered damage and casualties. But *Clematis*, a mercifully small target, was unharmed. She survived many more adventures but none so remarkable as that Christmas morning. In his report on naval affairs to the Commons, A.V. Alexander, the First Lord of the Admiralty, mentioned the action adding that the signal by *Clematis* 'brought tears to his eyes.'
—Sir John Palmer, HMS *Clematis*

The de Havilland DH98 Mosquito multi-role combat aircraft.

The U.S. Liberty ship, *Casimir Pulaski*, had a most interesting mixed cargo: military ambulances on deck, Chesterfield cigarettes in one hold, small arms ammunition in another, Dole pineapple juice in another and, finally, phosgene gas in the last hold. This was the only freighter on which I slept with a gas mask suspended over my head. Apparently the gas was in case the Germans used it first, as they did in World War One. On this ship I saw one of the only two torpedoes that I saw during the war. Had it hit us, I think that the entire convoy would have been wiped out by the gas. An all-welded ship, the *Pulaski*'s welds started to crack just before the centrecastle. They were patched by the ship's carpenter with cement.
—Peter Macdonald, Able Seaman, Canadian Merchant Navy

Vital supplies being loaded aboard a cargo ship bound for Malta.

Malta

For 5,000 years, the Mediterranean has been the arena of great sea battles, and in World War Two that historic reputation did not change. When France collapsed in June 1940, the Italian dictator, Benito Mussolini, decided that the time had come when he could, with impunity, join Hitler in the war against the sole remaining member of the Western Allies. From that moment on, the little island of Malta was a highly vulnerable, isolated outpost of the British Empire, and a vital one. Without Malta, the Mediterranean could have been closed to Britain, and her armies in North and East Africa—the only land forces at that time able to engage the enemy—could have been faced with another, and more disastrous, Dunkirk.

The island's excellent harbour of Valetta, well-established airfield, and central position in the mid-east theatre, gave Malta a strategic importance out of all proportion to her size. The problem was that, even more than Britain, Malta needed a constant flow of imports to survive. She had no resources of oil or solid fuel, and very little grain. Even the forage for the goats which supplied the island's milk had to be imported. It was essential for what was to become known as "the classic convoy" to be instituted, and for Malta's reinforcement, code-named Operation Jaguar, to continue for so long as it was needed.

The nearest British bases were Gibraltar, a thousand miles to the west, and Alexandria, almost as distant in the east. The shipping routes from either direction were threatened by the Axis powers' air and sea bases in Sardinia and Tunisia to the west, and from Libya to the east, while Malta herself lay under direct threat from bombers based on Sicily, less than a hundred miles away. Malta's towns and facilities were bombed almost as often as those in southeast England, as were the ships in transit and in harbour. The danger from submarines and torpedo boats in the channel between the island of Pantelleria and the Cape Bon peninsula was particularly great, and all the more so when, as sometimes happened, the major Royal Navy escort vessels—the battleships, aircraft carriers, and heavy cruisers—had to be diverted to fight another battle or meet another threat.

In September 1940, the british Mediterranean Fleet was reinforced by the aircraft carrier HMS *Illustrious*, the battleship HMS *Valiant* and two anti-aircraft cruisers. Furthermore, a squadron of American Martin Maryland aircaft arrived on Malta to carry out reconnaissance flights over Italy. Two months later, Fairey Swordfish aircraft, flying off *Illustrious*, attacked Taranto harbour with bombs and torpedoes, sank three Italian battleships, damaged another, and destroyed the seaplane base. Then, the Germans took a hand. Fliegerkorps X were sent in from Norway with 300 aircraft—Ju 87 Stuka dive-bombers, Ju 88 bombers, Me 110 fighter-bombers and Me 109 fighters; ten U-boats were withdrawn from the Atlantic (to Admiral Dönitz's displeasure) to join the powerful, if variably effective, Italian underwater fleet. On 10 January 1941, Stukas hit *Illustrious* with six 1,000-pound bombs, and put her out of action; a few days later they did the same to *Furious*. Both carriers had to be withdrawn to America, for repair in Norfolk, Virginia.

Nevertheless, up to the end of 1941, most merchant ships continued to reach Malta safely, but in 1942 the situation changed. Between February and August, of eighty five merchantmen leaving British ports for Malta, twenty-four were sunk. In June, only two ships out of six that had sailed from the Clyde reached the island, where they were subjected to incessant bombing for the next fifty-four days. Still, the troopers, cargo ships and tankers set out on

Routine maintenance in wartime.

what was becoming known, not so much as the "classic", but as the "suicide" convoy.

In July 1942, a typical single cargo unloaded in the Grand Harbour of Valetta, during what was classified as Operation Tiger, consisted of guns and ammunition, cars and lorries, aviation fuel and spare parts for aircraft, wheat, flour and maize, cement, corned beef, and bales of cloth. The ship which carried that particular cargo was one of nine escorted by the battle-ship HMS *Nelson*, the aircraft carrier HMS *Ark Royal*, and other warships. Each master in the convoy, before sailing, had received this signal from the escort commander, Vice-Admiral Sir James Somerville: "For over twelve months Malta has resisted all attacks by the enemy. The gallantry displayed by her garrison and people has aroused admiration throughout the world. To enable this defence to continue it is essential that your ships, with their valuable cargoes, should arrive safely at the Grand Harbour . . . Remember, everyone, that the watchword is THE CONVOY MUST GO THROUGH."

As usual, the merchant skippers were told that they must not make smoke, that they must not show lights at night, and that, even in daylight, they must only use the dimmest lamps. If their ships were damaged, they must continue sailing at the best speed they could make. On the way to Gibraltar, they had practised evasive action, turning in unison, for two hours at a time, and every gunner had been given the chance to test his armament.

The Rock was blanketed in a fog when the convoy navigated the Straits of Gibraltar, and it was hard for the masters to maintain formation. The navigation lights of the *Port Chalmers*, carrying 2,000 tons of aviation petrol in four-gallon cans, were switched on at full power, and the *Deucalion*, sailing ahead, showed a cluster of cargo landing lights astern. Two days later, at nine-fifteen in the morning, nine aircraft, thought to be Italian, attacked, but no ship was hit. That evening, however, *Nelson, Ark Royal* and *Renown* sped away to the northeast, leaving the cruiser *Edinburgh* and the destroyers to escort the convoy.

Next day before the sun was up, a fleet of enemy torpedo boats attacked, and the escorting warships' searchlights lit the scene. "We saw an E-boat," said a merchant skipper, "and the cruiser let go with a broadside. When the spray subsided, the E-boat wasn't there." The attacks continued, on and off for thirty-six hours, during which time the seamen slept with their clothes on, if they slept at all, and subsisted on sandwiches and coffee. When they steamed into Valetta, they received the usual enthusiastic welcome from the islanders, crowded on the rocks and ramparts which made the harbour a natural arena, and General Sir William Dobbie, the governor of Malta, boarded every ship to shake the master's hand. In the fifteen days it took to unload the cargoes into lighters, the harbour was often under air attack, but the seamen stayed aboard their ships. They had brought in 58,000 tons of supplies, without a vessel lost, and were interested to learn, on the radio from Rome, that Mussolini's navy and air force claimed to have sunk a total of 70,000 tons.

That convoy may have been the last to reach Malta more or less intact—at least until May 1943, when the Allied armies drove the enemy out of North Africa. Between February and August 1942, of eighty-five merchantmen to set out for Malta, twenty-four were sunk and eleven had to abort the voyage and return to port. In terms of cargo, 43% of 314,690 tons from Britain, and 34% of 296,000 tons from Egypt, were lost. Few oil tankers got through in those months and most of the gasoline was carried by the cargo ships in drums and cans, and once it reached the island it was rapidly dispersed to maximise its survivability.

It was the islanders' steadfastness throughout the summer of 1942, when they were truly under siege, which earned Malta the George Cross—the civilian equivalent of the Victoria Cross. Some of the sharpest action came in August with Operation Pedestal, when a convoy of fourteen ships was two days' sailing eastward from Gibraltar. It included the *Port Chalmers, Deucalion,* and the *Melbourne Star*, all of which had sailed the route in the previous July, and the tanker *Ohio* carrying 11,000 tons of oil. The convoy's escort was of a strength which a merchant skipper on the North Atlantic route would only ever see in dreams. It consisted of the battleships *Nelson* and *Rodney*, the carriers *Victorious, Eagle, Indomitable* and *Furious* (loaded with Spitfires for Malta's defences), down. It blew me to the other end of the hangar, then the lift at that end copped it and I was thrown all the way back again. I was wearing steel helmet, flash gear and overalls, and I never had a scratch. That was that. Our combat air patrols had put up a terrific fight all day and shot down a lot of enemy aircraft, but now the black balls were out in the signals area, to show we couldn't fly, and we proceeded to damage control and fire-fighting as we turned for Gibraltar. All the way, this great lump that the bombs had torn out of the carrier's side from the bow back 120 feet, was stretching out at right angles and making a terrible noise like an aboriginal 'Didgery-doo'. That was all we could hear until we came into the Straits, and then it was the prisoners-of-war, Italian and German, who were filling up the holds of ships tied alongside, greeting us with shouts of 'Stuka, Stuka, Stuka.' We spent a while putting our casualties on board a trawler for an honourable burial at sea."

On 11 August, a German U-boat, *U73*, hit the aging *Eagle* with four torpedoes, and she heeled over, tipping her equally elderly aircraft overboard. One gallant pilot tried to take off on the sloping deck, but his aircraft slipped into the sea. Within seven minutes *Eagle* had turned over and gone down. Next day it was the turn of *Indomitable*, from whose deck the Hurricane pilots, waiting to be launched, had watched *Eagle*'s end. *Indomitable* was hit by bombs, and could no longer launch nor land her aircraft, but those already airborne landed on the flight deck of *Victorious* and continued operating. One merchant vessel had been hit, but she was still afloat.

On that day, 12 August, shortly before the battleships, the cruisers and Indomitable had turned back for Gibraltar, torpedoes from Italian submarines damaged two cruisers and sank an anti-aircraft cruiser. The convoy, with the destroyers and remaining cruisers, keeping close to the coast of Tunisia, sailed on to the southeast, and straight into the sights of the German E-boats. Four merchant ships and a cruiser went down. The Luftwaffe bombers, arriving with the dawn on 13 August, sank another merchant ship and damaged three more, including the *Deucalion*, which later sank. In the course of the day, the tanker *Ohio* was hit by a torpedo and three times by bombs, the third of which stopped her engines.

The *Melbourne Star*, meanwhile, with 4,000 tons of petrol, oil and lubricant aboard, plus 1,450 tons of high explosive, had narrowly avoided a collision during the mélée when the *Ohio* was first hit. Her master, Captain D.R. MacFarlane, found himself leading the convoy as it passed the lighthouse on Cape Bon. Then, he was overtaken by a destroyer, which led him through the minefields before forging on ahead. Having zig-zagged through a bright shower of shells and tracer bullets, MacFarlane regrouped with the convoy astern of *Waiwarama*, which was hit by a stick of bombs next morning and blew up. The *Melbourne Star* was showered with debris, and passed through what MacFarlane described as "a sea that was a sheet of fire". Her paintwork was burned away, and the bottoms of her lifeboats were reduced to charcoal. Thirty-six of her crew, seeing death by drowning as a better option than being burned alive, threw themselves into the sea (twenty-two were later rescued by a destroyer and the limping *Ohio*). It was not until she had docked in Valetta that a live six-inch shell was discovered, lodged between the deck planks and the steel ceiling of MacFarlane's day-room. (Sadly, on 2 April 1943, the *Melbourne Star* was sunk 500 miles southeast of Bermuda by torpedoes from *U129* while carrying a load of ammunition from Australia to Britain via the Panama Canal, and there were only four survivors).

On board the *Ohio*, the crew had somehow got the engines going, and she had rejoined the convoy, steaming at two knots, only to have the tail of a shot-down Stuka fall onto her poop deck. Throughout that morning, bombs exploded all around her; she was hit again, a fire broke out, and her engines stopped for good. The fire was partially extinguished, and she was taken in tow by HMS *Rye* with HMS *Penn* and HMS *Ledbury* on either side. With a great hole in her side, her forecastle awash, and fires breaking out from time to time, she was somehow tugged, pushed, and jostled for the last twenty miles into Valetta harbour. The Royal Navy had lost one cruiser, an anti-aircraft ship and a destroyer, with another cruiser and a carrier damaged. Nine merchantmen were down, five the victims of aircraft, four of E-boats, and 350 merchant seamen had been killed. But the cargoes of the four surviving vessels, and *Ohio*'s 11,000 tons of oil, marked the end of the siege of Malta, leading to the breaking of the Axis powers in Africa. Like the island, Captain D.W. Mason, master of the *Ohio*, was awarded the George Cross.

On 19 November 1943, the first convoy reached the Grand Harbour unopposed.

We were called to boat drill occasionally, which involved donning life-jackets and assembling on the boat deck. We called it 'Board of Trade Sports', and no-one took it very seriously. I can't recall ever seeing the lifeboats swung out when we were at sea, although they were, very occasionally, in port. The old type life-jackets with eight cork blocks were regarded as dangerous because they could break your neck when you jumped into the water. The old hands told us to jump carrying them. The kapok jackets with whistles and lights were a big improvement. It was remarkable that so many seafarers couldn't swim—they used to say 'no-one can swim a thousand miles'.
—Jack Armstrong, tanker steward, Merchant Navy

Flight deck personnel of the aircraft carrier HMS *Victorious* whose pilots fought to save a Malta-bound convoy on 22 August 1942.

Do not see danger everywhere and in everything, do not overestimate the enemy, do not always seek to place yourself in his position, do not assume that everything that is going on in the theater of war applies to yourself—these internal reservations and scruples are a sign of uncertainty, and of a negative attitude, which impairs your ability to reach a decision and endangers the success of the operations.

Audacity and a readiness to take responsibility, coupled with cool, clear thinking, are the pre-conditions and the basis of success.
—from *The U-boat Commander's Handbook*

Even wartime difficulties did not make me enjoy this method of serving oneself: pick up the tray, slide it along the bars, receive a slop of meat (not too bad, but a bit gristly), far too much potato and gravy and masses of cabbage . . . The coffee was vile, so I left.
—from *Mrs Milburn's Diaries: An Englishwoman's Day to Day Reflections* by Peter Donnelly

Even in peace, scant quiet is at sea; In war each revolution of the screw, each breath of air that blows the colours free, may be the last life movement known to you.

Death, thrusting up or down, may disunite spirit from body, purpose from the hull, With thunder, bringing leaving of the light, with lightning letting nothingness annul.

No rock, no danger, bears a warning sign, no lighthouse scatters welcome through the dark; above the sea, the bomb; afloat, the mine; beneath, the gangs of the torpedo-shark.

Year after year, with insufficient guard, often with none, you have adventured thus; some, reaching harbour, maimed and battle-scarred, some never more returning, lost to us.

But, if you 'scape, tomorrow, you will steer to peril once again, to bring us bread, to dare again, beneath the sky of fear, the moon-moved graveyard of your brothers dead.

You were salvation to the army lost, trapped, but for you, upon the Dunkirk beach; death barred the way to Russia, but you crosst; to Crete and Malta, but you succoured each.

Unrecognised, you put us in your debt; unthanked you enter, or escape, the grave;

Many aircraft of RAF Coastal Command and the Fleet Air Arm took part in the effort to escort and assist the convoy vessels through to Malta.

Whether your land remember or forget you saved the land, or died to try to save.
—For *All Seafarers* by John Masefield

We watched a fighter plane attempting to land on a merchant aircraft carrier in bad Atlantic weather. Twice the pilot had to abort, but somehow, on the third attempt, the ship was steady for seconds, and the plane landed just before she pitched and rolled again. We had prayed for that pilot, and our prayers were answered. It was a marvellous sight.
—William Bourner, 2nd Engineer, Merchant Navy

You may be sure we regard Malta as one of the master keys of the British Empire. We are sure that you are the man to hold it, and we will do everything in human power to give you the means.
—Prime Minister Winston S. Churchill, to the Governor of Malta, 6 June 1941

This much is certain; that he that commands the sea is at great liberty, and may take as much and as little of the war as he will.
—Francis Bacon

Normandy

D-Day: Any day marking a particularly important event or occasion. The term began to be used during World War One as a code designation for the Allied offensive at Saint-Mihiel. The most famous use of it, however, was in World War Two, when it designated the start of the Allied invasion of the Normandy coast. It originally was planned to be June 5, 1944, but was postponed until June 6 owing to bad weather. The "D" has no special significance, simply standing for "day", much as the "H" in H-Hour stands for "hour." However, one writer points out that all amphibious operations have a "departed date," for which D-Day may serve as an abbreviation.
—from *Fighting Words* by Christine Ammer

left: Canadian landing craft heading in to the Normandy beachhead on D-Day.

left: A FIJI-class British cruiser making a heavy smoke screen; right: American Rangers scaling the cliffs of Point du Hoc in Normandy on D-Day.

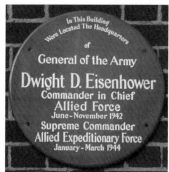

In This Building
Were Located The Headquarters
of
General of the Army
Dwight D. Eisenhower
Commander in Chief
Allied Force
June–November 1942
Supreme Commander
Allied Expeditionary Force
January–March 1944

top: Southwick Park, near
Portsmouth, was the operational
base of General Dwight Eisenhower
for the preparation and launch of
the Normandy invasion; left: The
London headquarters of SHAEF;
right: A memorial road marker near
the Normandy coast.

Every man in this Allied Command is quick to express his admiration for the loyalty, courage and fortitude of the officers and men of the Merchant Marine. To count upon their efficiency and their utter devotion to duty as we do our own; they have never failed us yet and in all the struggles yet to come we know that they will never be deterred by any danger, hardship or privation. When final victory is ours there is no organization that will share its credit more deservedly than the Merchant Marine.
—General Dwight D Eisenhower, London, June 1944

A German casemate gun emplacement at Longue sur Mer.

Empty and quiet, this stretch of
Omaha Beach offers few clues to
what happened here in June 1944.

Technically, destroyers have five different duties. First comes fleet work, for a battle fleet can never go to sea without destroyers as light covering forces. Then there is convoy work. Third comes defensive duties unsupported by bigger ships. Fourth, there is mine laying; and finally, the dozens of odd jobs, such as evacuation. It is a racketing life in destroyers, whether in the North Sea, the Channel, or the Atlantic. Off the East Coast there is never a let-up. The whole art of handling a destroyer successfully consists of seeing the other side first. It is most important, therefore, that glasses (binoculars) should be looked after with the greatest care. If dropped, they will go out of line. Usually they are cherished, and if anyone goes near the captain's glasses there is always likely to be trouble. The hardest job at the start of the war was undoubtedly convoy work. For months at a time individual destroyers would be fourteen days at sea with only forty-eight hours before going out again. They always had steam up, which reflected tremendous credit on the engineering side. Stokers were on watch month in and month out, and whereas the upper-deck crews were able to go on leave when the destroyer dropped her hook, the engine crews had to stay put.

—from *Life Line* by Charles Graves

above: The house which German Field Marshall Erwin Rommel used as his headquarters in Normandy in the time of the D-Day landings; far right: A German helmet recovered from Normandy.

The gallant Liberty ships brought food, equipment, ammunition, guns and other supplies to the Allied troops in southern England during the run-up to the Normandy Invasion in early 1944. After the landings, the Libertys busily shuttled between England and France, maintaining essential provisions to the beachhead.

Sailing aboard a Liberty offered considerable comfort. The officers' and crew's quarters were all in one house, eliminating the need for men to pass over weather decks to reach messes. Officers were able to retreat to private rooms; crewmen slept two or three to a room. Officers and crew ate at separate sittings, the officers in the 'saloon', the crew in another dining area. And one luxury for all were the showers, a great leap forward from the merchant seaman's traditional bucket-washings.
—from *Historic Ships of San Francisco* by Steven E. Levingston

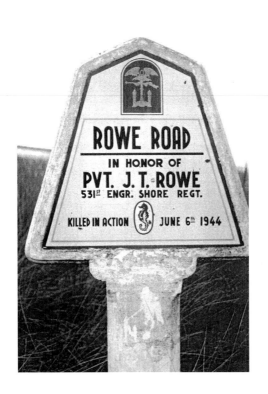

ROWE ROAD
IN HONOR OF
PVT. J. T. ROWE
531ˢᵗ ENGR. SHORE REGT.
KILLED IN ACTION   JUNE 6ᵗʰ 1944

Sᵗᵉ MERE-EGLISE
This was the first town
to be liberated
on the western front
5-6 June 1944

Saga of the all american

lower left: Utah Beach in 1990;
lower right: A German observation
post and firing position near
Arromanches.

Café Gondrée lies near Pegasus bridge, which was captured on 5 June 1944 by British glider forces to prevent German tanks attacking the Allies at Sword Beach.

above left: Britons entering Caen;
above: A German casemate in
Normandy; left to right: American,
British, and German military ceme-
teries, respectively, in Normandy.

Part of the giant U-boat pens at La Pallice / La Rochelle on the Brittany coast of France.

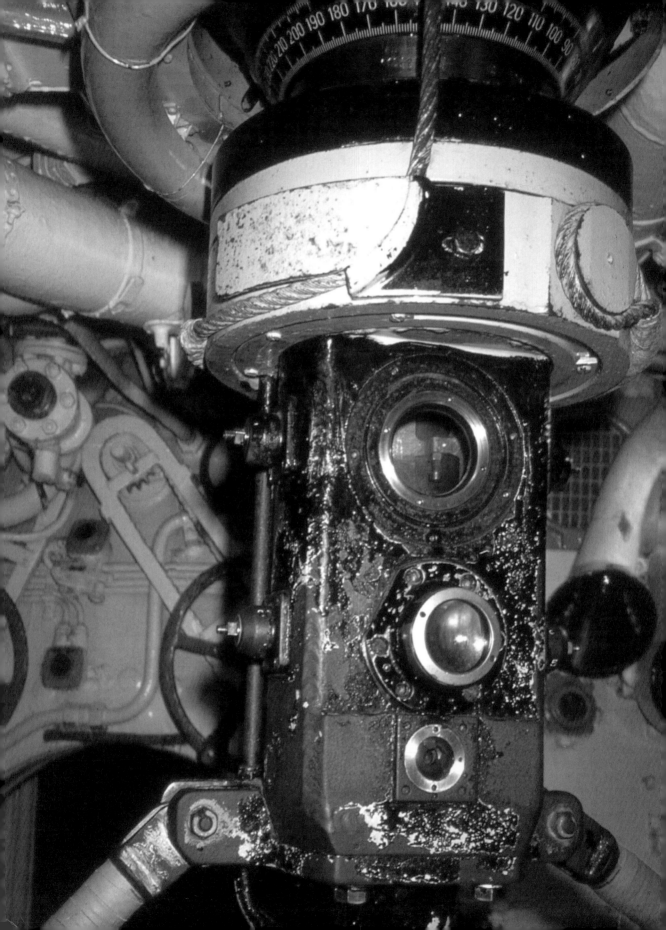

left: The periscope of *U-995*, a Type VIIC U-boat, now a museum at Laboe, Germany; below: The U-bunker at St Nazaire; bottom U-boat pens at Bordeaux, now part of the yacht marina.

123

The U-boat turntable and Dom bunkers at Lorient, as they appeared in 1990.

The Type VIIC U-boat *U-995*, restored to
function as a museum on the beach at Laboe
in northern Germany. It is the only surviving
Type VII.

The Seaman's Memorial at Halifax, Nova Scotia.